SEVENTH GRADE TECHNOLOGY

32 LESSONS EVERY SEVENTH GRADER CAN ACCOMPLISH ON A COMPUTER

FIRST EDITION

Part Eight of the Nine-volume Technology Curriculum by

Structured Learning LLC

First Edition 2013
Part Eight of Structured Learning's Technology Curriculum
Visit the companion website at http://askatechteacher.com for more resources to teach technology to children and online assistance with this textbook.

To receive free technology tips and websites, send an email to admin@structuredlearning.net with the message "Subscribe to Weekly Tips and Websites"

ISBN 978-0-9845881-9-0

Printed in the United States of America by Structured Learning LLC

Introduction

The educational paradigm has changed. New guidelines (most recently, the National Board of Governors Common Core Standards*) expect technology to *facilitate learning through collaboration, publishing, and transfer of knowledge*. Educators want students to use technology to *work together, share the products of their effort, and employ skills learned in other parts of their lives.*

How do we as teachers facilitate collaboration-publishing-transfer of knowledge?

We do it with the Structured Learning K-8 Technology Curriculum as roadmap. Aligned with Common Core State Standards and National Educational Technology Standards, and using a time-proven method honed in classrooms, students learn the technology that promotes literacy, critical thinking, problem-solving, and decision-making. The purpose is not to teach step-by-step computer skills (like adding borders, formatting, creating a blog). There are many fine books for that. What this curriculum does is **prepare students for their future**. If technology education doesn't serve life goals, it's not relevant.

> *"The significant problems we face cannot be solved at the same level of thinking we were at when we created them."*
>
> *- Albert Einstein*

Note: If there are skills you as teacher don't know, visit AskATechTeacher.com for free assistance. It is staffed by tech teachers ready to help you.

What's in the Seventh Grade Technology Curriculum?

Here's a quick overview of what you will find in this textbook:

- *Themed units that tie into inquiry, including problem solving, logical thinking and digital citizenship*
- *Articles on tech pedagogy*
- *Scope and Sequence—aligned with ISTE and Common Core*
- *Experiential learning with real-world applications*
- *Opportunities for students to express and grow in their creativity*
- *International mindedness*

Each Unit includes:

- *Common Core Standards with emphasis on comprehension, problem-solving, critical thinking, **preparing students for career and college***
- *ISTE Standards*
- *essential question*
- *big idea*
- *materials required*

- *time required to complete*
- *vocabulary used*
- *problem solving*
- *steps to accomplish goals*
- *assessment strategies*
- *ways to extend learning*
- *project examples where appropriate*
- *grading rubrics where appropriate*

How to Use This Book

Here are a few hints on how to use this curriculum effectively in your classroom:

- Units focus on school inquiry, collaboration and sharing, and strategies to be used throughout student learning career.
- Units use the 'flipped classroom' approach to teaching. Homework prepares students so class time can be spent on enrichment.
- A lesson is forty-five minutes. A Unit is two lessons. Some units, like Google Earth, require multiple weeks.
- Always use lesson vocabulary. Students learn by your example.
- 'Teacher Preparation' often includes chatting with subject teachers so you tie into their inquiry.
- Check off each item in Unit lesson plan as it is completed. Go back to those you don't complete when you have time.
- Check off each item in Scope and Sequence as it is completed.
- Some Scope and Sequence entries link to Common Core standards where you can get more detail.
- Expect students to be risk takers. Don't rush in to solve their problems. Ask them to think how it was done in the past or what strategies might provide a solution. Focus on problems listed in the Unit, but embrace all that come your way.
- The curriculum tries to use free and equitable software and web-based tools. If there are programs you can't access, email us and we'll help you develop a work-around.
- We understand what happens when kids and technology collide—sparks. Sometimes you can't move on because students are too excited about what they're doing. Take an extra week. Most school years run 35+ weeks. This book includes 32 units.
- If you have the print version and need a link, Google the name. If that doesn't work, visit our Help blog (http://askatechteacher.wordpress.com) and ask the teacher there for the link. If s/he is too slow (which s/he won't be), email Zeke.Rowe@structuredlearning.net with the name, textbook, page number. He'll track it down.

> *Civilization advances by extending the number of important operations which we can perform without thinking of them.*
>
> *--Alfred North Whitehead*

The table below outlines what's covered in grades six through eight. Where topics are taught multiple years, teaching reflects increasingly less scaffolding:

	Vocab	Problem-solving	Windows	KB	MS Office	Google Earth	Search/Research	Visual Learning	Pro-gram'g	WWW	Robotics	Games	Dig Cit
6	☺	☺	☺	☺	☺	☺	☺	☺		☺			☺
7	☺	☺		☺	☺	☺	☺	☺	☺	☺	☺	☺	☺
8	☺	☺		☺	☺	☺	☺	☺	☺	☺	☺	☺	☺

Copyrights

About the Authors

Structured Learning IT Team *is the premier provider of technology instruction books and ebooks to education professionals including curricula, how-to guides, theme-based books, and one-of-a-kind online help—all to fulfill the tech demands of the 21st century classroom. Materials are classroom-tested, teacher-approved with easy-to-understand directions supported by online materials, websites, blogs, and wikis. Whether you are a new teacher wanting to do it right or a veteran educator looking for updated materials,* **Structured Learning** *and its team of technology teachers is here to assist.*

Ask a Tech Teacher *is a group of technology teachers who run an award-winning resource* **blog** *where they provide free materials, advice, lesson plans, pedagogic conversation, website reviews, and more to all who drop by. The free newsletters and website articles help thousands of teachers, homeschoolers, and those serious about finding the best way to maneuver the minefields of technology in education.*

TABLE OF CONTENTS

Grades 6-8 Scope and Sequence

Units:

Arranged by theme:

Search/Research

Programming

Collaborate/Publish/Present

Articles

1. 10 Things My Blog Taught Me
2. 10 Ways to be an Inquiry-based ...
3. 11 Ways to Make an Inquiry...
4. 13 Ways Twitter Improves ...
5. 14 Factors to Consider for Tech ...
6. 5 Must-have Skills for New Tech ...
7. 7 More Word Best Practices
8. 7 Digital Ways to End...
9. 7 Ways to Assess Student ...
10. Common Problems Students...
11. How to Integrate Web Tools into ...
12. How to Thrive as a Digital Citizen
13. Minecraft in School
14. PS
15. Secret to Teaching Tech: Delegate
16. What's a Digital Portfolio and ...
17. When is Typing Faster Than...
18. Where Can I Find Kid-safe ...
19. Will Texting Destroy Writing Skills?

6th-8th TECHNOLOGY SCOPE AND SEQUENCE©

Check each skill off with W/M/C as students accomplish it

('ISTE' refers to the ISTE Standard addressed by the skill)

Common Core Standards noted where appropriate

ISTE		*I-Introduced; W-Working on; M-Mastered; C-Completed*			
1		**Creativity and Innovation**	6	7	8
		Students demonstrate creative thinking, construct knowledge, develop innovative processes			
		Apply existing knowledge to generate new ideas, products, or processes	W	M	C
		Create original works as a means of personal or group expression	W	M	C
		Use models and simulations to explore complex systems and issues	W	M	C
		Contribute to project teams to produce original works or solve problems	W	M	C
		Learn to use multiple technology tools to create a final project	W	M	C
		Identify trends and forecast possibilities	W	M	C
		Graphics			
		Use software (i.e., Photoshop) and web-based tools as drawing platforms	W	M	C
		Know how to resize/move/crop an image	W	M	C
		Know how to add /format borders	W	M	C
		Know how to communicate text with images	W	M	C
		Know how to use a variety of online tools to create graphics	W	M	C
		Know how to share graphics with widgets, embed tools, screenshots	W	M	C
		Internet			
		Be comfortable using web-based tools	C	C	C
2		**Communication and Collaboration**			
		Students use digital media and environments to communicate/ work collaboratively, including at a distance, to support individual learning and contribute to the learning of others.			
		Interact, collaborate, and publish with peers, experts, or others employing a variety of digital environments and media	W	M	C
		Communicate information and ideas effectively to multiple audiences using a variety of media and formats	W	M	C
		Develop cultural understanding and global awareness by engaging with learners of other cultures	W	M	C

		Contribute to project teams to produce original works or solve problems	W	M	C
		Know how to Interact, collaborate, and publish with peers	W	M	C
		Understand the use of email, forums, etc., to communicate/collaborate	W	M	C
		Engage in collaborative discussions with diverse partners on grade-level topics,	W	M	C
		Use technology to produce/ publish writing and present relationships between information and ideas clearly and efficiently (CCSS.ELA-Literacy.WHST.6-8.6)	W	M	C
		Integrate information from different media to develop a coherent understanding of a topic or issue (CCSS.ELA-Literacy.RI.6.7)	W	M	C

Vocabulary

		Understand content-specific vocabulary	W	M	C
		Understand vocabulary relevant to programs students are using	W	M	C
		Understand vocabulary relevant to technology in general	W	M	C
		Consult reference materials, both print and digital, to research words being used in communication (CCSS.ELA-Literacy.L.8.4c)	W	M	C

Word Processing

		Know when to use a word processing tool to communicate	W	M	C
		Know how to use word processing programs both online and software, including Google Docs, Open Office, Word, and Text	W	M	C
		Use classroom principles of proper grammar, spelling	W	M	C
		Know how to use embedded link (Ctrl+Click)	W	M	C
		Know how to insert and format an object (table, chart, etc.)	W	M	C
		Know how to format a document	W	M	C
		Know how to insert a graphic organizer	W	M	C
		Know how to insert header, footer	W	M	C

Desktop Publishing

		Know when to use a desktop publishing program to share information	C		
		Know how to work with color schemes	C		
		Know how to make a magazine	C		
		Know how to plan a publication, including the use of Design Gallery	C		
		Know how to export a desktop publisher project to share in other formats	C		

Presentations

		Know when to use presentation software and widgets(i.e., PowerPoint)	C		
		Know how to auto-advance	C		

		Can share slideshow through web-based tools (like Issuu)	C		
		Include multimedia components (e.g., graphics, images, music, sound) and visual displays in presentations to clarify information (CCSS.ELA-Literacy.SL.6.5)	C		
		Present findings, use appropriate eye contact, adequate volume, and clear pronunciation (CCSS.ELA-Literacy.SL.7.)	C		
		Include multimedia components and visual displays in presentations to clarify claims and findings and emphasize salient points (CCSS.ELA-Literacy.SL.7.5)	C		
		Adapt speech to a variety of contexts and tasks, demonstrating command of formal English when indicated or appropriate (CCSS.ELA-Literacy.SL.7.6)	C		
Blogs					
		Interact, collaborate, publish with peers employing a variety of digital media	W	M	C
		Use blogs to develop cultural understanding by engaging with learners of other cultures	W	M	C
		Use blogs for journaling, reflection, tracking project progress	W	M	C
		Incorporate text, images, widgets to communicate ideas	W	M	C
		Contribute to project teams to produce original works or solve problems	W	M	C
		Follow rules for collegial discussions (CCSS.ELA-Literacy.SL.7.1b)	W	M	C
		Use blogs to engage effectively in collaborative discussions with diverse partners, building on others' ideas (CCSS.ELA-Literacy.SL.6.1)	W	M	C
		Use blogs to review key ideas and demonstrate understanding of multiple perspectives through reflection and paraphrasing (CCSS.ELA-Literacy.SL.6.1d)	W	M	C
		Use blogs to present findings, sequence ideas with pertinent descriptions, facts, and details to accentuate main ideas (CCSS.ELA-Literacy.SL.6.4)	W	M	C
		Pose questions that elicit elaboration and respond to others' comments with relevant ideas that bring discussion back on topic (CCSS.ELA-Literacy.SL.7.1c)	W	M	C
		Acknowledge new information expressed by others and, when warranted, modify their own views CCSS.ELA-Literacy.SL.7.1d)	W	M	C
		Write routinely for a range of discipline-specific tasks, purposes, and audiences (CCSS.ELA-Literacy.WHST.6-8.10	W	M	C
Spreadsheets					
		Know how to use a variety of spreadsheet program, online and software, to share knowledge	W	M	C
		Know how to sort data	W	M	C
		Use formulas to turn data into information	W	M	C
		Explore a business using models/simulations to study complex systems/issues	W	M	C
		Know how to create and format graphs	W	M	C
		Process data, report results by collecting data into Excel and reporting it	W	M	C
		Know how to share and publish Excel through a widget to blog and/or website	W	M	C
		Know how to use spreadsheets to reason abstractly and quantitatively (CCSS.Math.Practice.MP2)	W	M	C
		Know how to use spreadsheets to construct viable arguments (CCSS.Math.Practice.MP3)	W	M	C

			W	M	C
		Know how to use spreadsheets to Make sense of problems and persevere in solving them (CCSS.Math.Practice.MP1)	W	M	C
		Know how to use spreadsheets to model with mathematics (CCSS.Math.Practice.MP4)	W	M	C
		Look for and express regularity in repeated reasoning (CCSS.Math.Practice.MP8)	W	M	C

Visual Learning

			W	M	C
		Understand difference between sharing information textually and visually	W	M	C
		Understand how to blend graphics into a message	W	M	C
		Understand how to create/use graphic organizers (i.e., Venn Diagram)	W	M	C
		Know how to brainstorm collaboratively via a mind map	W	M	C
		Integrate quantitative or technical information textually and visually (e.g., flowchart, diagram, model, graph, or table).(CCSS.ELA-Literacy.RST.6-8.7)	W	M	C

Web-based tools

			W	M	C
		Communicate information, ideas effectively to multiple audiences using a variety of media, formats	W	M	C
		Introduce/use school technology for education, sharing, and collaboration	W	M	C
		Introduce Google Apps to assist students to thrive in the learning environment	W	M	C
		Know how to use cloud-based storage to assist collaboration	W	M	C
		Use web-based communication tools to share individual ideas	W	M	C
		Use models and simulations to explore complex systems and issues	W	M	C
		Learn a variety of tools by teaching them to classmates	W	M	C

3 Research and Information Fluency

Students apply digital tools to gather, evaluate, and use information

			W	M	C
		Evaluate and select information sources and digital tools based on appropriateness to specific tasks	W	M	C
		Plan strategies to guide inquiry by knowing how to choose links and menus and select the appropriate choice	W	M	C
		Locate, organize, analyze, evaluate, synthesize, and ethically use information from a variety of sources and media	W	M	C
		Know how to take internet notes for a project (i.e., Evernote)	W	M	C
		Integrate visual information (charts, graphs, photographs, videos, or maps) with other information in print and digital texts. (CCSS.ELA-Literacy.RH.6-8.7)	W	M	C
		Organize ideas, concepts, and information as appropriate to achieving purpose; include formatting, graphics, and multimedia CSS.ELA-Literacy.WHST.6-8.2a	W	M	C
		Conduct research to answer a question that allows for multiple avenues of exploration (CCSS.ELA-Literacy.WHST.6-8.7)	W	M	C
		Support claim(s) with credible sources; demonstrate understanding of topic or	W	M	C

		text (CCSS.ELA-Literacy.W.6.1b)			
		Draw evidence from informational texts to support analysis reflection, and research (CCSS.ELA-Literacy.WHST.6-8.9)	W	M	C
		Gather information from multiple digital sources, using effective search terms; citing credible sources, avoiding plagiarism (CCSS.ELA-Literacy.WHST.6-8.8)	W	M	C
		Compare and contrast information from experiments, simulations, video, or multimedia sources with that gained from text.(CCSS.ELA-Literacy.RST.6-8.9)	W	M	C
		Use technology to develop topic with well-chosen facts, definitions, concrete details, quotations, or other information (CCSS.ELA-Literacy.W.8.2b)	W	M	C
Internet					
		Understand how to be good digital citizens while visiting the internet	W	M	C
		Understand 'fair use', copyright, public domain	W	M	C
		Understand the impact of digital laws on consumer internet use	W	M	C
		Understand the complexities of digital commerce	W	M	C
		Understand the importance of a digital footprint	W	M	C
		Know how to evaluate the reliability and accuracy of websites	W	M	C
		Process data and report results using a variety of internet websites	W	M	C
		Use Web tools to enhance learning (i.e., QR codes)	W	M	C
		Search for text on a page with Ctrl+F	W	M	C
		Evaluate search result before clicking link	W	M	C
		Know how to use online tools to guide inquiry	W	M	C
		Understand the unique purpose played by social media in communicating	W	M	C
Google Earth					
		Know when to use Google Earth to explore a concept/share knowledge	W	M	C
		Be familiar with required tools	W	M	C
		Can get help via Google Earth help files, community, other	W	M	C
		Know how to save a picture and import into another tool	W	M	C
		Know how to process data and share results	W	M	C
		Can create, edit, and format placemarks	W	M	C
		Know how to use ruler to measure distances	W	M	C
		Can add image overlays in a Google Earth tour	W	M	C
		Can run a tour	W	M	C
		Can export Google Earth project to other formats for sharing	W	M	C

4	Critical thinking, Problem solving and Decision making			
	Students use critical thinking skills to plan and conduct research, manage projects, solve problems, and make informed decisions using appropriate digital tools and resources			
	Plan and manage activities to develop a solution or complete a project that coordinates with classroom units	W	M	C
	Able to transfer knowledge learned in technology to other classes, home	W	M	C
	Able to teach others a skill	W	M	C
	Use multiple processes, diverse perspectives to explore solutions	W	M	C
Critical thinking				
	Able to identify best solution to a problem	W	M	C
	Understand how to identify and define authentic problems and questions for investigation	W	M	C
	Always attempt to solve a problem before asking for assistance	W	M	C
	Know how to print to different locations	W	M	C
	Know how to save to network	W	M	C
	Can intuit how to use programs without being taught	W	M	C
	Know how to use simulations and games to develop critical thinking skills	W	M	C
	Can follow a multistep procedure when carrying out experiments, taking measurements, or performing technical tasks. (CCSS.ELA-Literacy.RST.6-8.3)	W	M	C
	Use technology to Introduce claim(s) and organize reasons and evidence (CCSS.ELA-Literacy.W.6.1a)	W	M	C
	Use technology to draw evidence from literary or informational texts to support analysis, reflection, and research (CCSS.ELA-Literacy.W.8.9)	W	M	C
	Interpret information from diverse media (visually, quantitatively, orally) and explain how it contributes to a topic, text, or issue (CCSS.ELA-Literacy.SL.6.2)	W	M	C
	Acknowledge and distinguish claim(s) from alternate or opposing claims, and organize reasons and evidence logically (CCSS.ELA-Literacy.WHST.6-8.1a)	W	M	C
	Use technology to compare reading a story to listening/viewing, contrasting what students "see" and "hear" to what they perceive (CCSS.ELA-Literacy.RL.6.7)	W	M	C
	Use technology to convey ideas, concepts, and information through selection, organization, and analysis of relevant content (CCSS.ELA-Literacy.W.8.2)	W	M	C
	Reason abstractly and quantitatively (CCSS.Math.Practice.MP2)	W	M	C
	Construct viable arguments; critique reasoning of others (CCSS.Math.Practice.MP3)	W	M	C
	Look for and make use of structure (CCSS.Math.Practice.MP7)	W	M	C
	Look for and express regularity in reasoning (CCSS.Math.Practice.MP8)	W	M	C
Problem solving				
	Identify and define authentic problems, questions for investigation	W	M	C
	Accept responsibility for solving a student's own problems	W	M	C

		Can trouble shoot a non-working program	W	M	C
		Know keyboard shortcuts as alternatives for menu items	W	M	C
		Can solve most common computer problems without adult assistance	W	M	C
		Can learn new tech skills by reflecting on past knowledge	W	M	C
		Know how to access work from anywhere in the school (digital portfolios)	W	M	C
		Attend to precision (*CCSS.Math.Practice.MP6*)	W	M	C
		Make sense of problems and persevere in solving them (*CCSS.Math.Practice.MP1*)	W	M	C

Decision Making

		Know which program is right for what task	W	M	C
		Identify and define authentic problems and questions for investigation	W	M	C
		Collect, analyze data to identify solutions and make informed decisions	W	M	C
		Evaluate advantages/ disadvantages of different mediums (e.g., print, digital, text, video, multimedia) to present a topic or idea (*CCSS.ELA-Literacy.RI.8.*)	W	M	C
		Use appropriate tools strategically (*CCSS.Math.Practice.MP5*)	W	M	C

Pre-programming (With Scratch and Alice)

		Apply existing knowledge to generate new ideas, products, or processes	W	M	C
		Create/add/edit characters	W	M	C
		Add sound	W	M	C
		Add text bubbles	W	M	C
		Add backgrounds	W	M	C
		Add movement	W	M	C
		Complete program task cards of most common skills	W	M	C
		Broadcast	W	M	C
		Use models created by others; remix to develop unique programs	W	M	C
		Make sense of problems and persevere in solving them (*CCSS.Math.Practice.MP1*)	W	M	C
		Reason abstractly and quantitatively (*CCSS.Math.Practice.MP2*)	W	M	C
		Construct viable argument and critique reasoning of others (*CCSS.Math.Practice.MP3*)	W	M	C
		Model program with mathematics (*CCSS.Math.Practice.MP4*)	W	M	C
		Use appropriate tools strategically (*CCSS.Math.Practice.MP5*)	W	M	C
		Attend to precision (*CCSS.Math.Practice.MP6*)	W	M	C

		Look for and make use of structure(CCSS.Math.Practice.MP7)	W	M	C
		Look for and express regularity in repeated reasoning (CCSS.Math.Practice.MP8)	W	M	C
	Robotics				
		Contribute to project teams to produce original works or solve problems	W	M	C
		Build a robot	W	M	C
		Program a robot to perform necessary tasks	W	M	C
		Trouble shoot problems	W	M	C
		Use sensors to monitor environment	W	M	C
		Measure distances with robots	W	M	C
	Gaming				
		Understand how decision making is required to solve problems	W	M	C
		Use gaming to nurture thinking, reasoning, creativity, and collaboration	W	M	C
		Use gaming to develop and test hypotheses	W	M	C
		Use gaming to encourage collaborative work, negotiate social agreements	W	M	C
		Use gaming to learn principles of math science, and more	W	M	C
5	**Digital citizenship**				
	Students understand human, cultural, societal issues related to technology/practice legal and ethical behavior				
		Exhibit a positive attitude toward technology that supports collaboration learning, and productivity	W	M	C
	Computers and Society				
		Advocate and practice safe, legal, and responsible use of information	W	M	C
		Introduce the concept of 'digital citizenship'	W	M	C
		Understand how to create a good digital footprint	W	M	C
		Know how to safely use social media	W	M	C
		Understand netiquette expected of digital citizens	W	M	C
		Use and recognize safe, responsible and ethical behavior on the internet	W	M	C
		Demonstrate personal responsibility for lifelong learning	W	M	C
		Set the standard for digital citizenship among classmates	W	M	C
		Use the 'cloud' to extend learning	W	M	C
		Understand responsibility for avoiding and preventing cyberbullying	W	M	C

		Know how to respect the need for privacy online	W	M	C
		Gather information from multiple digital sources, using effective search terms; citing credible sources, avoiding plagiarism (CCSS.ELA-Literacy.WHST.6-8.8)	W	M	C

6 Technology operations and concepts

Students demonstrate a sound understanding of technology concepts, systems, and operations

		Understand and use technology systems	W	M	C
		Select and use applications effectively and productively	W	M	C
		Use school technology and digital media strategically and capably	W	M	C
		Transfer current knowledge to learning of new technologies	W	M	C

Hardware

		Understand how parts of computer connect	W	M	C
		Understand terminology for all computer hardware	W	M	C
		Understand which devices are for input and output and why	W	M	C

Keyboarding

		Know how to use keyboarding software	W	M	C
		Know how to use keyboarding internet sites	W	M	C
		Attain grade-appropriate speed and accuracy goals	W	M	C
		Can touch type	W	M	C
		Can compose at keyboard by creating classroom-based projects	W	M	C
		Understand how fast student can write vs. keyboard	W	M	C
		Use curved hand, reach, correct hand, finger reach	W	M	C
		Use correct posture, elbows at sides	W	M	C
		Know parts of keyboard—keys, numbers, F keys, arrows, Esc	W	M	C
		Use technology to produce/publish writing, collaborate with others (CCSS.ELA-Literacy.W.6.6)	W	M	C
		Demonstrate sufficient command of keyboarding skills to type a minimum of three pages in a single sitting (CCSS.ELA-Literacy.W.6.6)	W	M	C

Windows

		Know how to use Windows to run a slideshow of images	W	M	C
		Understand how to add file folders	W	M	C
		Know desktop, task bar, clock, start button	W	M	C
		Know how to use tool tips (hover over icon)	W	M	C

	Understand how to add file folders		W	M	C
	Understand right-click menus		W	M	C
	Know how to copy-paste between programs		W	M	C
	Use 'snipping tool' to collect information		W	M	C
	Know how to drag-drop between folders		W	M	C
	Know how to access different drives from Explorer or 'Computer'		W	M	C
Web-based Tools Student Can Use					
	Blogs		W	M	C
	Calendar (web-based)		W	M	C
	Digital portfolio		W	M	C
	Dropbox		W	M	C
	Email		W	M	C
	Google Apps (or similar)		W	M	C
	Internet Start Page		W	M	C
	Texting		W	M	C
	Twitter		W	M	C
	Website		W	M	C
	Wikis		W	M	C

Unit 1—Introduction

Vocabulary	Problem solving	Big Idea
• *Back-up* • *Digital* • *Digital citizen* • *Input* • *Landscape* • *Multimedia* • *Operating system* • *Orientation* • *Output* • *PC* • *Portrait* • *Programming* • *Robotics* • *Scratch* • *Select-do* • *Technology* • *Visual learning*	• *When do I 'save' and when 'save-as'?* • *I can't find file (start button>search)* • *I'm not allowed to use technology (tech is much more than the internet)* • *Computer doesn't work (how have you fixed this in the past?)* • *Plan didn't work (Troubleshoot it, then move onto the next plan)* • *What's 'see the forest for the trees' mean?* • *I don't have an email account (use parents? Does the school have student accounts?)* • *What's 'select do' (you must select before you 'do' to something)* • *How do I preview unit for homework? (watch video; review materials; record your questions)*	***Students understand the part technology plays in education***
Time Required *90 minutes*	**NETS-S Standards** *2a, 6a*	**CCSS** *Anchor standards*

Essential Question
How do I use technology?

Overview

Materials

Internet, online poll, posters on walls

Teacher Preparation

- Make sure school portal works for all student tech tool log-ins
- Have poll created and embedded into class website, blog, or other
- Have notes online for students to preview upcoming unit
- Have Tech Tips posters on classroom walls
- Talk with classroom teacher so you tie into their conversations.
- Test equipment to insure it works

Steps

_____Tour classroom to introduce students to the place they'll learn in twice a week. Where are the tech tools that will assist them? Printer? Tech devices? Announcements? Class internet start page? Blogs? Websites? What else?

_____Review class rules with students (see example at end of Unit—'Computer Lab Manners and Responsibilities'). Collect more from students, including:

- *No excuses; don't blame people; don't blame the computer.*
- *Save early, save often—about every ten minutes is a good time-frame*
- *No food or drink around computer. Period.*
- *Respect work of others and yourself.*
- *Keep hands to yourself—feel free to help a neighbor, but with words, not by doing for them.*
- *When engaging in collaborative discussions (one-on-one, in groups, and teacher-led), build on others' ideas and clearly express your own (from Common Core Standards CCSS.ELA-Literacy.SL.7.1).*

_____Introduce technology. What does it mean at your school? Where are your students in their understanding of tech in education? How have they used it? Take as long as necessary to complete this conversation.

_____Discuss the focus of 7th grade technology:

Best Practices

- *Technology is a tool to extend education*
- *Learning includes thinking, problem solving, know how to logically move from A to Z*
- *Learning is student-centric with teacher as guide*
- *Units are flipped—students review material as homework and practice during class*

1. **Think critically:**
   - *which program, tools and strategies work best for what activity*
   - *devise solutions to problems based on past knowledge*
   - *trouble-shoot; find alternatives*
   - *work collaboratively to draw on everyone's knowledge*
   - *understand what you do and don't know, and the difference*
   - *research answers effectively, efficiently, and ethically*
2. **Employ problem solving skills:**
   - *use available tools to solve a problem*
   - *critically think about a problem; ignore chaff; focus on pertinent details*
   - *present information in a way others understand*
   - *make sense of data*
3. **Transfer knowledge:**
   - *...to other parts of academic and social life*
   - *publish and share online as a means of collaborating, seeking criticism*
   - *create a digital portfolio accessible from many locations.*
   - *link information to others*
4. **Be a good digital citizenship:**
   - *learn to thrive in the digital world*
   - *learn fundamentals of research, search, social media, communication*
   - *understand rights and responsibilities inherent to digital world and those who inhabit it*
5. **Learn fundamental tech skills:**

- *learn to type faster than you can think*
- *know how to word process in various programs (i.e., Word, Google Docs, Text, Open Office, blogs, forums)*
- *use spreadsheets to turn data into information*
- *make presentations that are efficient, effective, and interesting*
- *understand tech hardware and how to trouble shoot when needed*
- *learn digital devices needed to thrive in the learning community*
- *know what online tools are available and what they can be used for*

_____Review Table of Contents with students. This year, class is less about tech skills and more about higher order thinking. Notice the arrangement of units by theme. Do students see relationships:

- *Basics—what tools are available to enhance learning? Why is keyboarding important? Why is it important to understand tech terminology? How can understanding hardware help students use tech efficiently and with less problems?*
- *Logical thinking—How can technology help solve problems? Why is visual learning a critical alternative to textual learning? How can robotics, programming, games show how to recognize/solve problems?*
- *Productivity software—Do students learn Microsoft Word/Excel (word processing and spreadsheets) or are they learning how to select the right tool for a need?*
- *Digital citizenship—How much time do students spend on the internet? How can that time be more productive? What are internet community rules? What are the rights and responsibilities students must consider before crossing the digital boundary?*
- *Search/Research—How does one sort through the millions of bits of online information to find answers?*
- *Programming—What if the answer has never been invented?*
- *Collaborate/Publish/Present—How can collaborating, publishing, and sharing benefit everyone? Why is it important to transfer knowledge from the classroom to life?*

_____Review Homework Policy—due monthly via email, dropbox, or other (not printed). Most often, homework will be what students didn't finish during class, preview of next class unit, and keyboard practice.

_____Discuss student responsibility to make up missed classes.

_____Review Hardware:

- *Mouse buttons—left and right, double click, mouse wheel*
- *CPU—power button, CD drive, USB port, plugs*
- *Monitor—power button, screen, station number*
- *Headphones—volume, size adjustment, connection to CPU*
- *Keyboard—home row, F-row, arrows, number pad*

_____Review how parts connect—behind CPU, under table, in front ports. Review whether parts are 'INPUT' or 'OUTPUT'. What's that mean?

_____Review 'save' and 'save-as' rules. Review when to use 'delete' or 'backspace'.

_____Review 'Select-Do' (see poster on next pages). What does that mean (you must select something before you can do to it)?

_____Before class ends, bring up on SmartScreen a poll created (on PollDaddy or similar) and embedded into class website/wiki/blog. It lists 7th grade topics (you may want to only include what's covered in the grading period):

- *Review each unit briefly with students. 'Sell" it as exciting and useful.*
- *Ask students to vote on which unit they think will be the most fun, most useful, or most exciting to learn.*
- *Don't tell how to find poll other than where it is located. Let them be explorers and risk-takers as they dig through school digital tools.*
- *Leave poll open until next class.*
- *Take another poll at end of year/grading period and compare results.*

_____As you teach, incorporate lesson vocabulary.

_____Throughout class, check for understanding. Expect students to solve problems and make decisions.

_____Remind students to transfer knowledge to classroom or home.

_____Tuck chairs under desk, headphones over tower; leave station as it was.

Assessment Strategies
- *Anecdotal*
- *Followed Common Core listening/speaking skills*
- *Joined class discussions*

Extension:
- *Students who finish visit class internet start page for websites that support inquiry. See more detail on that in next unit.*
- *Homework: Find and take poll.*
- *Homework: Preview school tech tools in preparation for next unit (flip classroom).*
- *Homework: Practice keyboarding on assigned website (i.e., Typing Web).*

More Information:
- *Lesson questions? Go to http://askatechteacher.com*
- *For ideas on assessing students, see article at end of unit on "7 Ways to Assess Student Knowledge"*

- *For ideas on inquiry-based classrooms, see article at end of unit on "10 Ways to be an Inquiry-based Teacher"*
- *For ideas on how to create an inquiry-based classroom, see article at end of unit on "11 Ways to Make an Inquiry based Classroom"*

If you don't get through everything, check completed items so you know what to get back to when you have time on later lessons. I find as I focus on the central idea of a lesson, clarifying questions sometimes take more time than I'd expect. I'm fine with that. There'll be lessons later that move faster than planned.

"The full use of your powers along lines of excellence."

- definition of "happiness" by John F. Kennedy

Computer Lab Manners

and

Responsibilities

Assignments / Homework

- Check class website each day.
- Read and respond to email daily.
- If an assignment is not completed in class, turn it in remotely from home by 6:00 pm the same day with no penalty.
- Late assignments are 10% off for each day late.

Behavior in the Lab

- Keep an open mind that *something new will be learned* each day.
- Have clean hands; keyboards are shared by everyone.
- No food or drinks allowed in lab
- When helping other students, use words. Do not take over their computer.

Emails and Posting Online

- Always enter subject of email
- Start each email with a greeting. (e.g. Hi Mrs. *** or Dear Mr. ***)
- Use correct punctuation. Start sentence with a capital; end with a period.
- Proof read email and check spelling.
- Show insight and intelligence when responding to a class discussion or commenting on a post.
- CC anyone mentioned in an email. That's polite
- Don't share private information in emails. They aren't secure!
- Don't be rude in emails.
- Don't use capitals—THIS IS SHOUTING
- More hints under Week #2

7 Ways to Assess Student Knowledge

This is always challenging, isn't it? Finding evidence that students have learned what you taught, that they can apply their knowledge to complex problems. How do you do this? Rubrics? Group projects? Posters? None sound worthy of the Common Core educational environ—and too often, students have figured out how to deliver within these guidelines while on auto-pilot.

Where can we find authentic assessments that are measurable yet student-centered, promote risk-taking by student and teacher alike, are inquiry-driven, and encourage students to take responsibility for his/her own learning? How do we assess a lesson plan in a manner that insures students have learned what they need to apply to life, to new circumstances they will face when no teacher is at their elbow to nudge them the right direction?

Here are some of my favorite approaches:

Anecdotally

I observe their actions, their work, the way they are learning the skills I'm teaching. Are they engaged, making their best effort? Do they remember skills taught in prior weeks and apply them? Do they self-assess and make corrections as needed?

Transfer of knowledge

Can students transfer knowledge learned in my class to other classes and/or other parts of their life? Do I hear fun stories from parents and teachers about how students used something learned? Do the students themselves share a snippet about how they 'helped mom use Google Maps to find..."

Teach others

Are students comfortable flipping learning and becoming the teacher? There's a hierarchy of learning that goes like this:

1. *Student doesn't listen*
2. *Student doesn't believe*
3. *Student tries it once*
4. *Student remembers it*
5. *Student shows it to others*
6. *Student teaches others*

Like Maslow's Hierarchy of Needs, the highest praise is that students teach the skill to others. That's learning.

I encourage it in my classes by having the lab open during recess and lunch, but with students as helpers. I only take 1-2 and always have more offers than I need.

Verbalize

Can students use the right words to share answers? No umms, no hand motions, no giggles. Can they take a deep breath and share their knowledge in a few succinct sentences? This works well on a Discussion Board which I use as a summative for vocabulary and problem solving tests. I set up a discussion board, ask each student to add a problem or vocabulary word we covered, and then comment on a classmate's. They can then use this resource during the test. We've done it a few times and students have figured out if they blow off the Discussion Board part of the assessment, everyone suffers. Friends don't have the study guide, or worse, the answer's wrong because classmates didn't take the time to write it correctly.

Portfolio

I like portfolios, but today, that means digital. Collect all student work onto wikis, digital lockers, Box.net, via embed widgets or screen shots or the original software. Keep it in the cloud where students, teachers, even parents can access it. That's transparency. No one will wonder what grade the student earned

Summarize knowledge

But not in an essay. Use knowledge to create a magazine, an Animoto video, a Puzzlemaker crossword (click Great Resources for ideas). It's the 'use' part of assessment that's most important. Can students use the knowledge or does it just sit in a mental file folder?

Oral presentations

This can be summative, formative, informational, or informal. It can be a quick answer to questions in the classroom, coming up to the SmartScreen and solving a problem, teaching classmates how to solve a problem during class, or preparing a multimedia presentation to share with others online or in person. It includes much more than an assessment of learning. It judges a student's presentation skills, ability to talk to people—life skills fundamental.

In the end, the choice of assessment depends upon the goal of teaching. Which works best for you?

10 Ways to be an Inquiry-based Teacher

It's hard to run an inquiry-based classroom. Don't go into this teaching style thinking all you do is ask questions and observe answers. You have to listen with all of your senses, pause and respond to what you heard (not what you wanted to hear), keep your eye on the Big Ideas as you facilitate learning, value everyone's contribution, be aware of the energy of the class and step in when needed, step aside when required. You aren't a Teacher, rather a guide. You and the class move from question to knowledge together.

Because everyone learns differently.

Where your teacher credential classes taught you to use a textbook, now it's one of many resources. Sure, it nicely organizes knowledge week-by-week, but in an inquiry-based classroom, you may know where you're going, but not quite how you'll get there—and that's a good thing. You are no longer your mother's teacher who stood in front of rows of students and pointed to the blackboard. You operate well outside your teaching comfort zone as you try out a flipped classroom and the gamification of education and are thrilled with the results.

And then there's the issue of assessment. What students accomplish can no longer neatly be summed up by a multiple choice test. When you review what you thought would assess learning (back when you designed the unit), none measure the organic conversations the class had about deep subjects, the risk-taking they engaged in to arrive at answers, the authentic knowledge transfer that popped up independently of your class time. You realize you must open your mind to learning that occurred that you never taught—never saw coming in the weeks you stood amongst your students guiding their education.

Let me digress. I visited the Soviet Union (back when it was one nation) and dropped in on a classroom where students were inculcated with how things must be done. It was a polite, respectful, ordered experience, but without cerebral energy, replete of enthusiasm for the joy of learning, and lacking the wow factor of students independently figuring out how to do something. Seeing the end of that powerful nation, I arrived at different conclusions than the politicians and the economists. I saw a nation starved to death for creativity. Without that ethereal trait, learning didn't transfer. Without transfer, life required increasingly more scaffolding and prompting until it collapsed in on itself like a hollowed out orange.

So how do you create the inquiry-based classroom? Here's advice from a few of my efriend teachers:

1. *ask open-ended questions and be open-minded about conclusions*
2. *provide hands-on experiences*
3. *use groups to foster learning*
4. *encourage self-paced learning. Be open to the student who learns less but deeper as much as the student who learns a wider breadth*
5. *differentiate instruction. Everyone learns in their own way*
6. *look for evidence of learning in unusual places. It may be from the child with his/her hand up, but it may also be from the learner who teaches mom how to use email*
7. *understand 'assessment' comes in many shapes. It may be a summative quiz, a formative simulation, a rubric, or a game that requires knowledge to succeed. It may be anecdotal or peer-to-peer. Whatever approach shows students are transferring knowledge from your classroom to life is a legitimate assessment*
8. *be flexible. Class won't always (probably never) go as your mind's eye saw it. That's OK. Learn with students. Observe their progress and adapt to their path.*
9. *give up the idea that teaching requires control. Refer to #8—Be flexible*
10. *facilitate student learning in a way that works for them. Trust that they will come up with the questions required to reach the Big Ideas*

In the end, know that inquiry-based teaching is not about learning for the moment. You're creating life-long learners, the individuals who will solve the world's problems in ten years. Your job is to ensure they are ready.

11 Ways to Make an Inquiry-based Classroom

You became a teacher not to pontificate to trusting minds, but to teach children how to succeed as adults. That idealism infused every class in your credential program and only took a slight bump during your student teacher days. That educator, you figured, was a dinosaur. You'd never teach to the test or lecture for forty minutes of a forty-five minute class.

Then you got a job and reality struck. You had lesson plans to get through, standards to assess, and state-wide tests that students must do well on or you'd get the blame. A glance in the mirror said you were becoming that teacher you hated in school. You considered leaving the profession.

Until the inquiry-based classroom arrived where teaching's goal was not the solution to a problem, but the path followed. It's what you'd hoped to do long ago when you started—but how do you turn a traditional entrenched classroom into one that's inquiry-based?

One step at a time, and here are fifteen you can take. One or more will resonate with your teaching style:

Flip the classroom

The night prior to the lesson, have students read the lecture materials so you can spend class time in hands-on discovery.

Don't answer student questions—show them how to do it themselves.

When students have questions, you guide them toward answers. Don't give them a fish, rather teach them to fish. When students understand the methodology, they can repeat the process. Without understanding, they are robots.

But this requires comprehensive teacher preparation to be ready for the multitude of directions a conversation can go, not just steer student inquiry where you're comfortable. Inquiry-based lessons are process-, not product-oriented. How students reach conclusions is as important as the conclusions they reach. That critical thinking is what it's about. Think back to your favorite school lessons. Were they where you learned the capital of every state or where you came to understand the scientific method? (OK, maybe that comparison doesn't work, but you get my point—likely, your favorite lessons required you to think, not regurgitate).

Listen when students speak

It's tempting to think you know what students are going to ask/say. Resist the impulse. Listen. Try to understand what their real question is, not what their words say. Watch them. Are they comfortable with your answer, or does it make them squirm? Take the time to travel the distance to a solution.

Encourage questions.

Class is ticking away and there are too many questions. If you take time to answer all of them, you won't cover the material scheduled.

That's OK. Take the time. Make the issues clear. An odd thing will start to happen. As students more thoroughly understand a concept, they will transfer that knowledge to other lessons and those will go faster than expected. By the end of the year, you'll have covered more material in more depth. Cool, hunh?

Spend time on projects, not lecturing

There's an old Chinese proverb, although Ben Franklin occasionally gets credit for these words:

> *"Tell me and I'll forget.*
> *Show me and I may remember.*
> *Involve me and I'll understand."*

Inquiry is about doing, not observing, action not inaction.

Lessons are fluid

Learning isn't linear. It's a web that grows out from the central question. As such, your lesson plan may change dramatically based on student inquiry. If you teach three fifth grade classes, each will likely be different from the other. That's OK. Your challenge is to track what you did in each class and pick up from where you left off. That's OK, too. It's part of the job of teaching an inquiry-based class.

Publish and share

Inquiry-based classrooms share knowledge. This can be accomplished via a class wiki, blogs, websites, but it's done. Students understand how to embed articles and projects into the internet or class network so its shared by everyone. They accept that part of their responsibility as a student is to ask questions about these shared materials, read and comment on them, and use them as resources. We all grow when one grows.

Reflection is included in every lesson plan

What did students learn? Where can they transfer it? You as teacher do that after every teaching experience. Your students do it also. Then you understand if what they learned was what you planned. Or something else.

You are a fellow learner

Students learn they are valued in the classroom experience. Their conclusions bend discussion, mold learning. In this way, they understand the importance of their participation in projects, reflections, and collaborative experiences. Encourage this. Accept that the inquiry-based classroom will be noisier than the typical class—and that's a good thing.

Questions don't have yes-no answers

Likely, they don't even have a concrete answer. They are more 'how' and 'why', which requires investigation into multiple strands to answer well. Assessment, then, becomes the student ability to use problem-solving and thinking skills, not to repeat someone else's conclusions.

Summative assessments are less paper-and-pencil and more hands-on, creative, student-centered

They are less about answering teacher questions than sharing student learning. You might even have students create their own assessments in something like PuzzleMaker.

That's it—eleven ideas. Any handful of these approaches will morph your classroom from passive to sparkling, from boring to brilliant. In the comments, share what happened the first time you tried to remove the pedagogic anchor and set your class lose, the simple goal: learning?

Unit 2—Digital Tools

Vocabulary	Problem solving	Big Idea
• *Blog* • *Cloud* • *Digital locker* • *Digital portfolio* • *Doc* • *Dropbox* • *Embed* • *Gmail* • *Internet start page* • *Mash-up* • *Network* • *Portfolio* • *Tweet* • *Twitter* • *Weblog* • *Widget* • *Wiki*	• *Computer crashed? Remind students: Save early save often.* • *Log-in didn't work? Look up UN/PW (from wherever they saved it)* • *Computer doesn't work (check power)* • *Can't find tool (right click or try shortkeys)* • *Can't put class calendar on my blog (check Google Calendar embed info)* • *Can't put class calendar on internet start page (check instructions—try email address)* • *Doc is too large to email (save to email 'Drafts')* • *How do I rename a folder?*	***Students develop an awareness of digital tools that support and enhance education***
Time Required *90 minutes*	**NETS-S Standards** *2b, 5b*	**CCSS** *Anchor standards*

Essential Question
How do I share my knowledge with classmates?

Overview

Materials
Internet, student blog set-ups, student Google Apps set-up, student dropboxes (if available), class internet start page, student digital portfolios (network folders, Google cloud, or what your school uses), class Twitter account, class wiki accounts

Teacher Preparation
- Have log-ins to school keyboarding program available for students (if required)
- Have notes online for students to preview upcoming unit
- Have class wiki page fleshed out
- Have class blog set up with associated student blogs if required
- Have class internet start page filled with relevant detail (including daily *To Do*)
- Test heading macro to be sure shortkey is not used for another function
- Have student network folders available
- Talk with classroom teacher so you tie into their conversations

Steps

_____**Required skill level for this unit: No special knowledge.**

_____Any questions from homework (review of school digital tools)? Expect students to have reviewed upcoming unit and have questions. Prod if necessary.

_____Next week: Speed quiz. This will be a benchmark. Add it to class online calendar. Remind students where this is or have a student come up to SmartScreen and show classmates how to find it.

_____Discuss results of interest poll.

_____Discuss digital tools in general terms. What are they? How are they different from software and/or apps? Which ones have students used? Why have they become mainstays in education? See if students come up with ideas such as:

- *to facilitate collaborative work*
- *to enable students easily publish and share a project with classmates*
- *to make communication with multiple audiences easier*
- *to enable use of a wide variety of media and formats*
- *to encourage cultural understanding and global awareness*
- *to provide options (for example: communication options—email, forums, blogs)*
- *to provide access from anywhere with an internet connection*

_____This Digital Tools unit has three goals:

- *introduce digital tools used in 7th grade*
- *acclimate students to the concept that as a learner, tech tools enable differentiation, collaboration, sharing, and publishing—goals supported by Common Core and ISTE*
- *show how to employ them in student educational endeavors*

_____Discuss goals of school's technology (from Common Core):

- *to serve student education goals*
- *to promote learning strategically and capably*

_____Discuss digital citizenship in broad strokes. You focus on it in Unit 10-12 and return to it every time students use internet. Remind students of rights and responsibilities inherent to the digital community.

_____Here's a list of the most common digital tools used in schools. Review those that apply to your situation and add any not included:

- blogs
- online calendar
- class internet start page
- digital portfolios (aka 'digital lockers')
- email
- Google Apps
- homework dropbox
- iPads
- network folders (if no digital portfolios)
- Twitter
- websites—teacher and student
- wikis

Blogs

_____Introduce 'blogging'—articles published online, enhanced with images or videos that engage readers in a conversation. No software to install or keep up to date. No IT glitches.

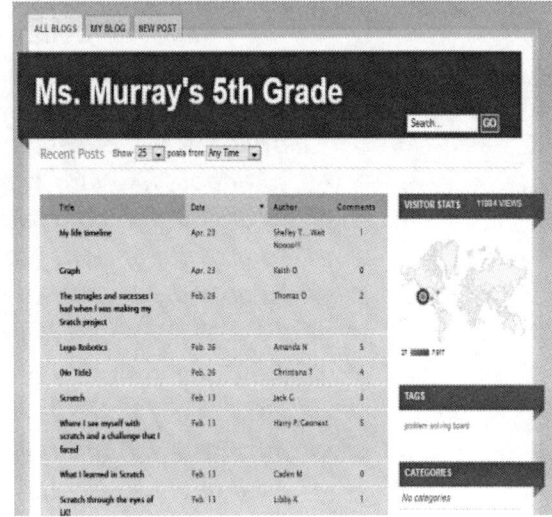

_____Studies show blogs attract a wider audience than traditional reading venues, improve student writing while making it fun and hip, incorporate discovery into education, and draw learners into self-guided discussions. Blogs give ownership of content to students.

_____Teachers can use blogs to:

- *pose questions and require students respond to classmate comments*
- *pose hypotheses that ask students to present findings and sequence ideas with descriptions, facts, details*
- *review key ideas*
- *ask students to demonstrate understanding of multiple perspectives*
- *engage students in collaborative discussions, building on others' ideas*
- *encourage students to acknowledge new information expressed by others and, when warranted, modify their own views*

_____Before beginning, discuss blog netiquette: Be polite, use good grammar and spelling, don't say anything you don't want everyone to read (school blogs are traditionally private, but get students used to the oxymoron of privacy and the internet).

_____Have students sign onto class blog account. There are several popular options—like Edublogs, Class Blogmeister, Blogger (the latter comes with Google Apps)—but I use KidBlogs. It is set up by teacher and requires no student sign-up or email (click for links).

_____Students can create a profile picture with an avatar creator like (click for link, Google for address, or use your favorite):

- *Clay yourself*
- *Monster yourself*
- *Lego you*
- *Animal yourself*
- *Make me a hero*
- *Madmen yourself*
- *Voki yourself*

_____Show students your personal or professional blog. Have entries that tie into class inquiry. Ask students to comment on one. Encourage students to respond to classmate comments and ask/answer questions.

_____After students set up their blog, have them write about themselves. Only provide information they are comfortable sharing. Include images, video, and/or music as needed.

_____Remind students to practice good keyboarding habits as they type—posture, hand position, etc.

_____Ask students to comment on five classmate blogs. Be supportive, extend the conversation, share knowledge, ask questions. Follow rules of collegial discussion (see Common Core SL.7.1b). Use comments to modify thinking if appropriate.

_____Once a month, students post an article that reviews key ideas about a topic being discussed. Demonstrate understanding of multiple perspectives through reflection and paraphrasing and by answering comments of classmates. Alternatively, post may present findings and sequence ideas with pertinent descriptions, facts, and details. It should elicit responses from classmates with a goal of building a better understanding of the concept.

_____Encourage students to include text, images, widgets in their posts.

_____Occasionally, have students blog as a team on original content of their choosing, with a goal of engaging classmates in a discussion.

Class Calendar

_____Create calendar (through Google Apps or other) and embed into class website or wiki. List project due dates, home-work, quizzes. Code events by color if possible. Send notifications to student email and/or Smartphones.

_____Students can embed into their blogs and/or wiki pages for a greater reach. Show students how to edit calendar.

Encourage students to contribute.

_____For training on how to use Google Calendar, click
http://edutraining.googleapps.com/Training-Home/module-3-calendar).

_____Demonstrate by adding next week's keyboarding speed quiz and homework while
students observe.

Class Internet Start Page

_____An internet start page is the first page that comes up when students select the
internet icon. Its purpose in education is to make internet use simple and safe for students.

_____Include everything students visit on a daily basis (i.e., class guidelines, calendar, daily 'to do' list, typing websites, research locations, sponge sites, a calculator) as well as information specific to current project.

_____Mine also includes pictures of interest, rss feeds of interest, weather, news, a graffiti wall, and class pet dog. Yours will be different.

_____I used protopage.com, but you can use netvibes, pageflakes.com (Google for
addresses), or another. Each comes with a collection of widgets to personalize page
to specific needs.

_____When you get class page set up, include student start-up tasks for each class while
you wrap something else up.

Digital Portfolios

_____Students use Digital Portfolios (also known as digital lockers) to:

- *store work (in the Cloud) required in other classes or at home*
- *interact, collaborate, and publish with peers, experts, or others*
- *contribute to project teams*
- *edit or review work in multiple locations*
- *submit class assignments (for paper free schools)*

_____There are a variety of approaches to creating digital portfolios that satisfy some or all
of the above uses: 1) folders on school network, 2) fee-based programs from companies such as Richer Picture or Teacher Web, 3) cloud-based storage like Dropbox or
Google Apps, and 4) online collaborative sites like Wikispaces or PBWorks,

_____You can use a combination of these options, also. Where student network folders are
great for storing files, Google Docs and wikis are better at collaborating/interacting

with classmates. Choose what works best for your students. The more options, the better, so students get familiar with a variety of tools.

_____Here, we use a combination of Google Apps (discussed later in this Unit because it serves many purposes beyond a digital portfolio) and a wiki.

_____What is a 'wiki'? What's it mean to be edited 'by the people'? Most students are familiar with 'Wikipedia' but few know they can join/edit this popular online encyclopedia.

_____Have a Wikispace page set up for class. Include information on:

- *Purpose of wiki*
- *Wiki rules*
- *How students get started*
- *How to use as a Digital Portfolio*
- *Where students get help*
- *Where students find their pages*
- *Other important info*

_____Tour the wiki with students, focusing on:

- *How privacy is maintained (no last names; inherent wiki security precautions). Circle back on previous discussions about digital citizenship, digital security and digital footprints. Answer any questions. Take time for this, especially if online communication is new to students.*
- *Sidebar—where students find important topics, links to class assignments, links to student personal pages, and items of importance to your unique student group.*
- *Top pop-out toolbar (log-in, messages received, personal avatar)*
- *How students add their page.*
- *How students have a discussion.*
- *How to edit (and when they can't, i.e., page is 'locked').*

_____Take questions, then have students set up a Wikispaces account and join class wiki. This is student-directed as much as possible.

_____Have students create their page. Use a template you created (I call mine 'student template'—see inset) which includes information such as: 1) student name and avatar, 2) headings for each project, 3) Table of Contents, and 4) whatever makes wiki useful.

_____Remind students to use good grammar and spelling on anything going on the internet. This is part of their digital footprint (circle back on prior discussions of this topic) and should be as impressive as possible. College is right around the temporal corner!

_____Once students create a page, link it to class list of student pages so it's easily located.

_____Create an avatar using an online creator (see 'Blogs' for suggestions)

_____Those who finish can visit classmate pages and comment using *Discussions* icon.

_____Several times throughout the year, assess digital portfolios. There are rubrics <u>here</u> and <u>here</u> or Google 'eportfolio rubric'. Mash up one to suit your needs.

Email

_____Use web-based email accounts (i.e., Gmail) or Gmail accounts that come with Google Apps for Education.

_____Discuss email rules on poster at end of unit (see inset). Do students have other suggestions?

_____Review email basics—*To, cc, subject line, body of email, attachment, urgent*—then have students create an email and send it to you to confirm your address and theirs.

_____Discuss how email accounts can be used as a back-up for important documents (by emailing a copy to themselves or creating a draft email with doc attached and stored in email 'Draft' file).

EMAIL ETIQUETTE

1. Use proper formatting, spelling, grammar
2. CC anyone you mention
3. Subject line is what your email discusses
4. Answer swiftly
5. Re-read email before sending
6. Don't use capitals—THIS IS SHOUTING
7. Don't leave out the subject line
8. Don't attach unnecessary files
9. Don't overuse high priority
10. Don't email confidential information
11. Don't email offensive remarks
12. Don't forward chain letters or spam
13. Don't open attachments from strangers

Google Apps

_____Google Apps for Education has more than 20 million educational users. The suite of (free) tools includes:

- *Gmail (for email)*
- *Google Drive (for word processing, spreadsheets, presentations, forms)*
- *Cloud storage (in Google Drive)*
- *Google Calendar*
- *Google Sites (websites)*
- *Google Groups*
- *Google Contacts*

_____Everything created in Google Apps is backed up instantly in the Cloud, secure and private. Importantly, it enables collaboration and sharing anywhere—two cornerstones to Common Core and ISTE. This facilitates a shift from MS Office's software-based, print-centric programs to a more open, equitable and green approach to education (Microsoft now has their version called Office 365).

_____Click here for Google training for Google Apps. Click here for student training.

_____Show students how to get started on student accounts—log in, use Drive, share documents with others, more. Demonstrate similarity between Google Docs/Spreadsheet/Presentation and MS Office.

Homework dropbox

_____A homework dropbox can be through the school website account (i.e., Schoology), email, or Google Apps (through the 'share' function). I've even used a Discussion Board. This encourages collaboration and feedback while honing writing and thinking skills. Any alternative to printed homework submitted via an inbox is a good thing.

_____If your school has this option, review so students are comfortable with its usage.

_____If you have Google Apps, you can create a Homework dropbox like this:

* *Each student creates a folder called 'Dropbox' that is shared with you*
* *Every time they want to submit work to you, they copy/move it to that folder so you can view and comment*

Ipads

_____Many students are familiar with iPads so start by asking what they know and what's their favorite iPad use? As they share, demonstrate and have students try them.

_____If your students are unfamiliar with this exciting tool, start with an introduction, iPad in-hand. Take a tour of the screen (apps, task bar, search function revealed with right swipe), home button, recharger (make it student responsibility to put it back into iPad cart plugged into charger), front and back camera, microphone, jack (for headphones—critical with 20 students in a room, all using iPads), on/off, volume, the dock. Show students how to check battery to be sure they have enough.

_____Brainstorm for best practices using iPads in a classroom, proper care, what students can do but shouldn't at school (i.e., don't change settings or delete apps or change wallpaper).

_____Show students how to save images to iPad from Google or Google Apps. Discuss digital rights and privacy.

_____Every new tech appliance needs a killer app, and iPads have theirs—running apps. Thousands—tens of thousands—of them, each with a particular corner on creativity and ingenuity. Let students explore the apps you installed.

_____If you want activities to familiarize students with the iPad, click here (http://wp.me/pySW5-2vX)

Network Folders

_____If students don't have Google Drive accounts, set up student folders on school network. Discuss the meaning of 'network'—accessible from anywhere in school, but not off campus.

_____Discuss passwords and the importance of privacy. Do not share log-ins with anyone.

_____Have students save log in info in their school binders or wherever it is secure.

_____Have students create folders in their network folder for each class they are taking.

Class Twitter account

_____Twitter is a natural in the 7th grade classroom. It is hip. Students want to check their stream to see what's up. Because tweets must be concise, they are an excellent way to teach writing.

_____Like blogs and wikis, Twitter feeds are used to:

- *engage effectively in collaborative discussions with diverse partners, building on others' ideas*
- *review key ideas and demonstrate understanding of multiple perspectives through reflection and paraphrasing*
- *present findings, sequence ideas with pertinent descriptions, facts, and details to accentuate main ideas*
- *Pose questions that elicit elaboration and respond to others' comments with relevant ideas that bring discussion back on topic*
- *acknowledge new information expressed by others and, when warranted, modify their own views*

_____Set up a private class twitter account for announcements, group questions, discussions that require collaboration. Use #hashtags to organize themes like #homework, #class, #questions, and whatever works for your student group.

_____Most blog and website activity can also be tweeted, so it's a great redundancy for getting news where it needs to go.

Student Websites

_____Available with Google Apps for Education, these are a great way to encourage reflection, organization, logical thinking, and a perfect place to embed sharable projects, i.e., Tagxedos, Animotos. If your school doesn't have Google Apps, free websites can be created at Weebly, Wix, or blog accounts like Wordpress.

_____Make website creation student-directed with you as facilitator. Encourage students to watch how-to videos and experiment with different tools and looks.

	1 Beginner	2 Capable	3 Accomplished	4 Expert
Quality of Writing	- Website has no style or voice - gives no new information on the topics - poorly organized	- Website has little style or voice - gives some new information on the topic - poorly organized	- written in a somewhat interesting style and voice - some new information on the topic or reflective - well organized	- written in an interesting style and voice - very informative or deeply reflective - well organized
Presen- tation	- many words misspelled - many grammar errors - formatting makes articles difficult to follow or read	- several spelling errors - several grammar errors - formatting makes website difficult to follow or read	- few spelling errors - few grammar errors - some formatting to help make the website easier to read	- all words spelled correctly - no grammar errors - formatting makes the post more interesting and easier to read
Design	- no multimedia, eye to layout and choice of colors, confusing to understand	- few pieces of multimedia, layout is sometimes effective, colors seem arbitrary	- mostly understandable, but looks amateurish though well-intentioned	- multiple pieces of multimedia, careful layout, colors add to communication, easy to follow
Community	- no links - post is not tagged or categorized --no way for readers to communicate with each other or creator	- one or more links - only "easy" links - articles may be categorized or tagged	- several links included that add to the reader's understanding - articles may be categorized or tagged	- several links to places that add to readers understanding - articles are fully categorized and tagged

_____Websites should reflect student personalities with colors, fonts, layout. Encourage creativity. What students include will help you better understand their interests, how they learn, and the best way to reach them academically.

_____You might ask students to theme their website—participate in something bigger than themselves, or inform readers of a personal interest topic. Decide what works best.

_____Occasionally (several times during grading period), assess development of websites with a rubric supplied to students. See inset and sample at end of Unit.

Teacher websites

_____Create a teacher website either through Google Sites or a free provider like Weebly, Wix, or blog accounts like Wordpress or Blogger. Use it to summarize class activities or a wider tech ed perspective. Mine is http://askatechteacher.com, to encourage students to learn technology.

_____Introduce it to students. Let them get to know you as a professional with a reach beyond school, as a star in your field.

_____Optionally, this can be school-focused with grade-level activities, parent resources, and extensions for interested students.

Class Wikis

_____Your classroom activities can be organized with blogs, internet start pages, wikis, twitter or all of them. Wikis (introduced under Digital Portfolios) are the most flexible and thorough. There can be pages for student and parent resources, monthly homework, What we did today (for absent students or interested parents), grade-level skills, favorite links—whatever you need. And, unlike blogs and internet start pages, students can participate in developing the site.

_____You may ask students to create their own wiki or just a class wiki page. Decide which serves your focus on:

- *Collaborating*
- *Sharing*
- *Showing evidence of learning*

_____Like blogs, wikis can be used to:

Assessment Strategies

- *Previewed material and came to class with questions*
- *Kept blogs, wikis, etc. up to date*
- *Transferred knowledge to projects*
- *Completed set-up projects*
- *Joined class discussions*

- *engage effectively in collaborative discussions with diverse partners, building on others' ideas (through Discussions)*
- *review key ideas and demonstrate understanding of multiple perspectives through reflection and paraphrasing*
- *present findings, sequence ideas with pertinent descriptions, facts, and details to accentuate main ideas*
- *pose questions that elicit elaboration and respond to others' comments with relevant ideas that bring discussion back on topic (through Discussions)*
- *acknowledge new information expressed by others and, when warranted, modify their own views*

_____Many wikis are free. I'll use <u>Wikispaces.com</u> in this example. If students are using wikis for digital portfolios, they are already set up. If not, show students how to create a Wikispace account, then join class wiki.

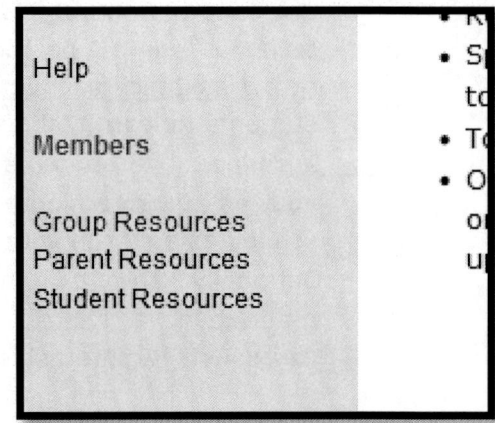

_____Have students add their first name (only) to 'Members' page on class wiki (see inset). Have a 'Student Template' that includes information you consider important, such as:

- *student name (first name and handle)*
- *student profile picture or avatar*
- *technology class journal*
- *help needed*

_____You can use avatars created under 'blogs' as profile picture.

_____Remind students to transfer knowledge to classroom or home.

_____Tuck chairs under desk, headphones over tower; leave station as it was.

_____As you teach, incorporate lesson vocabulary.

Extension:
- *Create Vokis as an introduction to student wiki or blog.*
- *Create a <u>Tagxedo</u> on what students think about technology, what tools they're excited to learn, or a profile of themselves. Share on wiki, Site, or blog.*
- *Students who finish visit internet start page for websites aligned with class Inquiry.*
- *Homework: Set up all accounts as required to be prepared for next unit, including keyboard program (if that requires log-in). Add this to class calendar.*
- *Homework: Practice keyboarding to prepare for next week's Keyboarding unit. Add to class calendar.*

More Information:
- *Lesson questions? Go to http://askatechteacher.com*
- *See article at end of Unit on "How to Integrate Web Tools into the Classroom"*
- *See article at end of Unit on "What's a Digital Portfolio and Why Should You Use it?"*
- *See article at end of Unit on "10 Things My Blog Taught Me"*

- *See article at end of Unit on "13 ways Twitter Improves Education"*

If you don't get through everything, check completed items so you know what to get back to when you have time later. I find as I focus on the central idea of a lesson, clarifying questions sometimes take more time than I'd expect. I'm fine with that.

Sample Website Assessment Rubric

	1 Beginner	2 Capable	3 Mastered	4 Expert
Quality of Writing	- Website has no style or voice - gives no new information on the topics - poorly organized	- Website has little style or voice - gives some new information on the topic - poorly organized	- written in a somewhat interesting style and voice - some new information on the topic or reflective - well organized	- written in an interesting style and voice - very informative or deeply reflective - well organized
Presen-tation	- many words misspelled - many grammar errors - formatting makes articles difficult to follow or read	- several spelling errors - several grammar errors - formatting makes website difficult to follow or read	- few spelling errors - few grammar errors - some formatting to help make the website easier to read	- all words spelled correctly - no grammar errors - formatting makes the post more interesting and easier to read
Design	- no multimedia, eye to layout and choice of colors, confusing to understand	- few pieces of multimedia, layout is sometimes effective, colors seem arbitrary	- mostly understandable, but looks amateurish though well-intentioned	- multiple pieces of multimedia, careful layout, colors add to communication, easy to follow
Community	- no links - post not tagged or categorized —no way for readers to communicate with each other or creator	- one or more links - only "easy" links - articles may be categorized or tagged	- several links included that add to the reader's understanding - articles may be categorized or tagged	- several links to places that add to readers understanding - articles are fully categorized and tagged

EMAIL ETIQUETTE

1. Use proper formatting, spelling, grammar
2. CC anyone you mention
3. Subject line is what your email discusses
4. Answer swiftly
5. Re-read email before sending
6. Don't use capitals—THIS IS SHOUTING
7. Don't leave out the subject line
8. Don't attach unnecessary files
9. Don't overuse high priority
10. Don't email confidential information
11. Don't email offensive remarks
12. Don't forward chain letters or spam
13. Don't open attachments from strangers

How to Integrate Web Tools into the Classroom

'**Web 2.0**' is a term familiar to all teachers. Stated in its simplest form, it's the set of interactive internet-based tools used by students to enrich educational opportunities. '**Web 1.0**' referred to the act of accessing websites—nothing more. Students read websites, clicked a few links, and/or researched a topic. Web 2.0—Web-based education basics–includes blogs, wikis, class internet homepages, class internet start pages,

twitter, social bookmarks, podcasting, photo sharing, online docs, online calendars, even Second Life—all tools that require thoughtful interaction between the student and the site. For teachers, it's a challenge to keep up with the plethora of options as the creative minds of our new adults stretch the boundaries of what we can do on the internet. Students, adults, teachers who use this worldwide wealth of information and tools are referred to as 'digital citizens'. They leave a vast digital footprint and it is incumbent upon them to make healthy and safe decisions, including:

- *Treat others and their property with respect (for example, plagiarism—even undiscovered—is immoral and illegal)*
- *Act in a responsible manner*
- *Look after their own security*

Here are some activities you can do in your classroom that will make your lessons and activities more student-centered and more relevant to this new generation of students:

1. Create a **classroom blog**. Blogging has become one of the most effective learning tools in education. It introduces students to new methods of communicating, improves their writing, and motivates them to find their voice. You ask students about it, they'll tell you—blogs make learning fun. Click here for some examples.
2. Create a **classroom internet start page.** When students log onto the internet, have them bring up a start page with information relevant to them—targeted links, a To Do list, RSS feeds, search tools, email. Ask them what should be on it. Maybe they'd like sponge websites to fill extra minutes. Make it exciting! You might like one of these three templates to get you started:
   - Google Start Page
   - Protopage
   - Page Flakes
3. Each has a library of custom fields to individualize the start-up experience. Click here for my start page for K-8.
4. Build your own **classroom webpage**. Make it a learning portal open for business 24/7. Make sure it engages students while facilitating authentic real-world activities. You can make a free

page through <u>Scholastic</u>, <u>School Notes</u>, or <u>Google Sites</u>. Click here for examples of <u>school</u> <u>webpages</u>.

5. Create **online calendars** for students. These replace the traditional planners students carry to classes (and lose who knows where which becomes a traumatic event in young lives). Create your own on <u>Google Calendars</u> with viewing privileges for students and parents only, and then embed it into your class webpage, start page or wiki.

6. Create a **wiki**—a web page built by and for students. The most famous example is Wikipedia. Wikis can communicate school news, information on a research topic, terminology—whatever you want. For example, after teaching a lesson, have students go to the class wiki and summarize what they understood. Then, when test time arrives, students can study from everyone's notes. For examples, go to <u>Wikispaces for Educators</u>. I have one for every grade. Here's my <u>Year Six</u> (fifth grade in the USA) wiki.

7. Set up **social bookmarking** so students can save links to webpages they use for research, sports, music, and share them with others. Imagine the vast database you can compile by having students investigate a topic—say, the French Revolution—save the sites they visit to a group folder, and benefit from each other's research. What an amazing tool! Good options are <u>Diigo</u>, <u>Blinklist</u>, or <u>delicious</u>.

8. **Twitter** is a free social messaging utility that allows you to update parents and older students via short messages everyone will have time to read. In my case, I have one account for parents (it's private, so I won't share it here) and <u>one</u> for my PLN (personal learning network—I'd love to have you follow me). You can incorporate twitter widgets into webpages, add it to your Google desktop/ smartphone/ iPad, even your blog.

9. **Photo sharing** through <u>Flikr</u> or <u>Photobucket</u> (or others). Free online photo collections enable students/parents/teachers to share pictures from school events, sports and more. Students can search for photos to help with research (be sure to teach them correct annotations) and educators can upload photos for classes, school events, and more. At my school, students had to complete a photo journal after a field trip. Everyone uploaded their pictures, creating a huge pool to use for the follow-up project.

10. **Podcasting** is an efficient method of sharing lectures, instructions, and information. They appeal to those multi-intelligences that prefer visual and audio and can be replayed 24/7. With a nominal amount of equipment, anyone can create files and post them to the internet that can be accessed from a personal computer or handheld device. The most popular site is <u>YouTube</u>, but also try <u>TeacherTube</u>, <u>Vimeo</u>, and <u>EPN</u> (the Education Broadcast Network). For examples, visit <u>Small Voices</u> or <u>Webcast Academy</u>.

11. Everyone should try **online docs**. <u>Google Docs</u> has become the standard for free, easy-to-use document sharing at schools and can be limited to the school community of registered users. Even if you don't use it in your school, share it with parents. You'll be surprised how many will appreciate the alternative to MS Office.

Which others do you use to enhance and enrich your school teaching?
Photo credit: Johns Hopkins School of Education

What's a Digital Portfolio and Why Should You Use it?

By fifth grade, students have lots of school work that needs to be 1) saved for future use, 2) accessed from home and school, 3) shared with multiple students for collaborations, 4) linked to other pieces of work or online sites. For example, a student can create a project summary at school, access it at home and link key words to websites found by a classmate that supports the project discussion. As an educator, you might have goals for your class that aren't adequately fulfilled by network file folders or binders on a shelf in the classroom. You might be looking for ways to 1) help students become more reflective about themselves as learners, 2) demonstrate evidence of student growth and 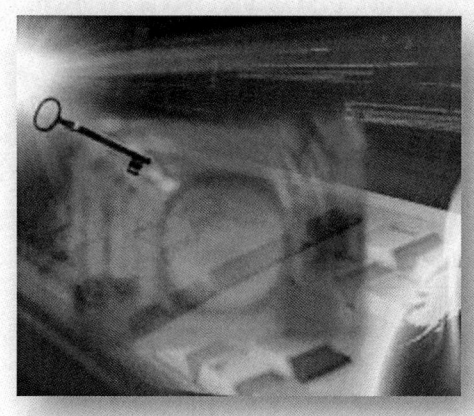 achievement, 3) inform instruction, influence practice, and set goals, 4) learn about your students, and 5) help students see technology as a tool rather than an end to itself.

This can all be accomplished with **Digital Portfolios**—also known as digital lockers or e-portfolios— *electronic collections of student work that provide evidence that the student is meeting a set of goals.*

The concept of digital portfolios is supported by national and international education pedagogy: 1) ISTE makes it important to "interact, collaborate, and publish with peers…" and "contribute to project teams to produce original works or solve problems", 2) the International Baccalaureate PYP program requires a digital portfolio be maintained throughout the student PYP school years, and 3) Common Core State Standards considers collaboration and publishing fundamental to accomplishing educational goals.

If you're new to digital portfolios, here are some Guidelines for Developing a Digital Portfolio Program from Todd Bergman, an educator who's helped hundreds of students create portfolios:

- *Be realistic about your design and expectations.*
- *Make use of relevant models.*
- *Instill a sense of ownership in students creating the portfolios.*
- *Communicate implementation strategies and timelines clearly.*
- *Be selective in design and strategy.*
- *Allow for continuous improvement and growth.*
- *Incorporate assessment stakeholders in all phases and components of your efforts; that is, make sure portfolio content meets the needs of those assessing the work.*

There are a variety of approaches to creating digital portfolios for fifth graders: 1) use file folders set aside on the school's network, 2) use fee-based software provided by companies such as Richer Picture, 3) use free online wikis. We will use a wiki—an online storage location/webpage with a dedicated page for each student.

Most students are familiar with 'Wikipedia' but few know they can join and edit this popular online encyclopedia. Wikis are websites edited 'by the people'. What's that mean for credibility?

Explain how the wiki pages we will use are secure and private. Circle back on previous discussions about digital citizenship, digital security and digital footprints. Discuss this with students. Answer any questions they may have.

There are a variety of wiki providers like Wikispaces and PBWorks. We'll use Wikispaces:

- Set up a Wikispace main account for each fifth grade class. Include information on (click for an example of my 5th grade wiki):

  - *What is a Wiki*
  - *What are this Wiki's rules*
  - *What does each student agree to when s/he uses this wiki*
  - *How do students get started*
  - *How do students use a Wiki as a Digital Portfolio*
  - *Where can users get help*
  - *Where are Student resources*
  - *Where can students find their pages*
  - *Where can students find Announcements*
  - *Is there a place for 'Extras'*

- Take most of one 45-minute class to introduce students to wikis, get them set up with Wikispaces and joined into the class wiki. Allow it to be student-directed as much as possible. Ask them to read the screen, and try to find solutions before asking for assistance. Most problems can be figured out with the application of brain power.
- Have students create their own page. Use a template you've created (I call mine 'student template') which includes the layout and critical information you want included. These might be: 1) an avatar, 2) headings for each project, 3) a Table of Contents, and 4) whatever else you want to highlight for your class.
- Remind students to always use good grammar and spelling on anything going on the internet. This is part of their digital footprint (circle back on prior discussions of this topic) and they want that as impressive as possible.

- Once students have created their page, have them link it to the generic 'student page' link on the class wiki so it's easy to locate.
- Now it's time to work on their digital portfolio. Start by personalizing it.
- Create an avatar using an online avatar creator (Clay yourself, a monster, Lego you, Wild animal, Make me a hero, Madmen yourself). Take a screen shot and upload it to the student wiki page. Demonstrate how students edit their page and then expect them to accomplish it.
- Next, create Vokis as an introduction to viewers of their wiki page. Provide guidelines as to what the Voki should say that fits your class. Show students how to use Wikispaces embed tool to place the interactive avatar on their website.
- Finally, create a Tagxedo discussing what students think about technology, what tools they're excited to learn, or maybe just a profile of themselves in word cloud format. When they've entered their words, picked their shape and fonts, show them how to 'share' by grabbing the embed code to insert into their Wiki page.

When these beginning steps are accomplished, give students time to visit each other's wiki pages and listen to the Voki greetings. Encourage them to leave comments using the Discussion tab.

Throughout the year, students will post their projects, both ongoing and finished. In some cases, they will collaborate with other students. Other times, they'll solicit feedback or reflect on what they have accomplished. It will vary with projects and you as the teacher will guide them with these goals.

Several times throughout the year, review portfolios in a more formal manner. There are several rubrics available (here and here or Google 'eportfolio rubrics') or create one that covers your particular needs.

10 Things My Blog Taught Me

When I started blogging, I wasn't sure where to take it. I knew I wanted to connect with other tech teachers so I used that as the theme. Now, thanks to the 491,000+ people who have visited, I know much more about the 'why'. It's about getting to know kindred souls, but there is so much more I've gotten from blogging. Like these:

How to write

I've learned to be frugal with my words. I choose verbiage that conveys more than one-word's-worth of information and I leave tangential issues for another post. Because I realize readers are consuming on the run, I make sure to be clear–no misplaced pronouns or fuzzy concepts like 'thing' or 'something'.

Prove my point

This part of writing transcends what print journalists must do. Yes, they do it, but my readers expect me to support ideas with interactive links to sources. If I'm reviewing a tech ed concept, I link to other websites for deeper reading. That's something that can't happen in paper writing. Sure, they can provide the link, but to put the paper down, open the laptop, copy that link–I mean, who does that? In a blog, I get annoyed if someone cites research and doesn't provide the link.

Listen

When I write an article, I cross post to other parts of my PLN, sometimes to ezines I contribute to in other parts of the world. And then I listen. What are readers saying? What are their comments/suggestions to me? Often, I learn as much from readers as what I thought I knew when I wrote the article.

How to work through the dry times

I rarely have writer's block, but when I do, I jump into the blogosphere and see what my colleagues are writing. In my fiction writing, I discovered that researching would water down the dry spells. The same thing works for blogging. I visit my favorite tech ed blogs, get inspired by their inspiration, research the pedagogy/topic, and often come up with my own take on it, based on my unique classroom experience.

How to persevere

Three years of blogging and I'm still waiting to make it big. What's that mean to me? I want that knock on my virtual door from **_Byte_** or **_PC Magazine_** asking me to come on board as a paid house blogger. Truth, that probably won't happen and by now, I've stuck it out so long I wouldn't know what to do if I stopped blogging.

How to market my writing

I try lots of ideas to market my writing, but thanks to the blogosphere, I know what everyone else is doing. I can try as much or little of it as I want. For me, I found a comfortable baseline and add a few pieces every year (this year, it's Pinterest).
One point worth mentioning is headlines. Usually, all I get from a reader is seven seconds–long enough to read the title, maybe the first line. If my title doesn't seem personal and relevant, potential readers move on. There are over <u>450 million English language blogs</u>. That's a lot of competition. I better hit a home run with the title.

There are lots of opinions out there

Often, I share my thoughts on the future or current status of tech ed. Sometimes, I'm surprised at comments I get. They might touch a corner of the idea I hadn't thought of or be 180 degrees from my conclusions. It forces me to think bigger as I write, consider how people who aren't me will read my words. That's both humbling and empowering. I think I'm much better at that than I used to be.

There are a lot of smart people in the world

In a previous lifetime when I built child care centers for a living, I read lots of data that said people thought the education system was broken–but not in their area. They considered themselves lucky because their schools worked. Well, as I meandered through life, I realized that applies to everything. People are happy with what they're comfortable with and frightened/suspicious of what they aren't used to. Through blogging, I get to delve into those ideas with them because we feel like friends. I've found that lots of people are smart, intuitive, engaged in life, looking to improve the world. I'm glad I learned that.

How to be responsible

Yes, blogging is demanding. I have to follow through on promises made in my blog profile and posts. When I say I'll offer tech tips weekly, I have to do that even if I'm tired or busy with other parts of my life. It's not as hard as it sounded when I first started. If you're a mom, you've got the mindset. Just apply it to blogging.

How to be a friend

My readers visit my posts and comment or poke me with a 'like'. Maybe, on my good days, they repost. Those are nice attaboys. I always return the favor by dropping by their blogs to see what they're up to, leave a comment on their latest article. It takes time, but like any relationship, is worth it. I have online friends I've never met who I feel closer to than half the people in my physical world. I've seen them struggle with cancer, new jobs, unemployment, kid problems. I've learned a lot about life from them.

13 Ways Twitter Improves Education

Twitter can easily be dismissed as a waste of time in the elementary school classroom. Students will get distracted. Students will see tweets they shouldn't at their age. How does one manage a room full of Tweeple without cell phones? Is it even appropriate for the lower grades?

Here's ammunition for what often turns into a pitched verbal brawl as well-intended teachers try to reach a compromise on Twitter (in fact, many of the new Web 2.0 tools—blogs, wikis, websites that require registrations and log-ins, discussion forums. You can probably add to this list) that works for all stakeholders:

You learn to be concise.

Twitter gives you only 140 characters to get the entire message across. *Letters, numbers, symbols, punctuation and spaces all count as characters on Twitter.* Wordiness doesn't work. Twitter counts every keystroke and won't publish anything with a minus in front of the word count.

At first blush, that seems impossible. It's not. True, you must know the right word for every situation. People with a big vocabulary are at an advantage because they don't use collections of little words to say what they mean, they jump right to it. All those hints your English teacher gave you–picture nouns and action verbs, get rid of adverbs and adjectives–take on new meaning to the Twitter aficionado.

Twitter isn't intimidating

A blank white page that holds hundreds of words, demanding you fill in each line margin to margin is intimidating. 140 characters isn't. Anyone can write 140 characters about any topic. Students write their 140 characters and more, learn to whittle back, leave out emotional words, adjectives and adverbs, pick better nouns and verbs because they need the room. Instead of worrying what they'll say on all those empty lines, they feel successful.

Students learn manners

Social networks are all about netiquette. People thank others for their assistance, ask politely for help, encourage contributions from others. Use this framework to teach students how to engage in a community—be it physical or virtual. It's all about manners.

Students learn to be focused

With only 140 characters, you can't get off topic. You have to save those for a different tweet. Tweeple like that trait in writers. They like to hear what your main topic is and hear your thoughts on it, not your meanderings. When you force yourself to write this way, you find it really doesn't take a paragraph to make a point. Use the right words, people get it. Consider that the average reader gives a story seven seconds before moving on. OK, yes, that's more than 140 characters, but not much.

Here's an idea. If you feel you must get into those off-topic thoughts. write them in a separate tweet.

Students learn to share

Start a tweet stream where students share research websites on a topic. Maybe the class is studying Ancient Greece. Have each student share their favorite website (using a #hashtag — maybe #ancientgreece) and create a resource others can use. Expand on that wonderful skill they learned in kindergarten about sharing their toys with others. Encourage them to RT posts that they found particularly relevant or helpful.

Writing short messages perfects the art of "headlining".

Writers call this the title. Bloggers and journalists call it the headline. Whatever the label, it has to be cogent and pithy enough to pull the audience in and make them read the article. That's a tweet.

Tweets need to be written knowing that tweeple can @reply

Yes. This is the world of social networks where people will read what you say and comment. That's a good thing. It's feedback and builds an online community, be it for socializing or school. Students learn to construct their arguments expecting others to respond, question, comment. Not only does this develop the skill of persuasive writing, students learn to have a thick skin, take comments with a grain of salt and two grains of aspirin.

#Hashmarks develop a community

Create #hashmarks to help students organize tweets: #help for a question, #homework for homework help. Establish class ones to deal with subjects that you as the teacher want students to address.

Students learn tolerance for all opinions

Why? Because Tweeple aren't afraid to voice their thoughts. They only have 140 characters—why not spit it right out. Because the Twitter stream is a public forum (in a classroom, the stream can be private, but still visible to all members of the class), students understand what they say is out there forever. That's daunting. Take the opportunity to teach students about their public profile. Represent themselves well with good grammar, good spelling, well-chosen tolerant ideas. Don't be emotional or spiteful because it can't be taken back. Rather than shying away from exposing students to the world at large, use Twitter to teach students how to live in a world.

Breaks down barriers to talking to other people

Students are less worried about typing 140 characters than raising their hand in class, all eyes on them, and having to spit out the right answer. With Twitter, students can type an answer, delete it, edit it, add to and detract from, all before they push send. Plus, it's more anonymous than the class, with no body language or facial expressions. Just words—and not many of those. Students have their say, see how others respond, have a chance to clarify. What could be safer.

Students are engaged

Twitter is exciting, new, hip. Students want to use it. It's not the boring worksheet. It's a way to engage students in ways that excite them.

Consider this: You're doing the lecture part of your teaching (we all have some of that), or you're walking the classroom helping where needed. Students can tweet questions that show up on the Smartboard. It's easy to see where everyone is getting stuck, which question is stumping them, and answer it in real time. The class barely slows down. Not only can you see where problems arise, students can provide instant feedback on material without disrupting the class. Three people can tweet at once while you talk/help.

Twitter, the Classroom Notepad

I tried this out after I read about it on Online Universities and turns out, it works as well for 8th graders as it does for higher education. Springboarding off student engagement, Twitter can act as your classroom notepad. Have students enter their thoughts, note, reactions while you talk. By the time class is done, the entire class has an overview of the conversation with extensions and connections that help everyone get more out of the time spent together.

Twitter is always open

Inspiration doesn't always strike in that 50-minute class period. Sometimes it's after class, after school, after dinner, even 11 at night. Twitter doesn't care. Whatever schedule is best for students to discover the answer, Twitter is there. If you post a tweet question and ask students to join the conversation, they will respond in the time frame that works best for them. I love that. That's a new set of rules for classroom participation, and these are student-centered, uninhibited by a subjective time period. Twitter doesn't even care if a student missed the class. S/he can catch up via tweets and then join in.

Please take a moment to vote in this poll. Tell me how you think Twitter would best benefit your classroom if you were using it.

Unit 3—Keyboarding

Vocabulary	Problem solving	Big Idea
• *Alt* • *Ctrl* • *F7* • *F row* • *Macros* • *Mulligan Rule* • *QWERTY* • *Reach* • *Shortkey* • *Touch typing* • *Word wrap* • *Wpm*	• *Cap doesn't work (Check caps lock)* • *What is today's date (Shift+Alt+D)* • *How do I exit a program (Alt+F4)* • *I can't find Word (use Search field)* • *I didn't do well on speed quiz (Mulligan Rule applies)* • *That quiz/test/project wasn't fair (Mulligan Rule applies)* • *I don't have time for homework (that's a choice, not a fact)* • *I can't think when I have to focus on key placement (practice more)*	*Work on essential elements of keyboarding—technique, speed, and accuracy—with grade level goals*
Time Required *90 minutes*	**NETS-S Standards** *3a, 6a*	**CCSS** *CCSS.ELA-Literacy.W.7.6*

Essential Question

How do I use technology to organize information faster and more efficiently?

Overview

Materials

Internet, keyboard program (software or online), speed quiz, word processing program, blank keyboard quizzes, handwriting quiz

Teacher Preparation

- Have Problem-Solving Board sign-up sheets on wall (if required)
- Have notes online for students to preview upcoming unit
- Ensure that all required links are on lab computer

Steps

_____**Required skill level for this unit: Student is familiar with keyboarding.**

_____Any questions from homework (review of keyboarding curriculum)? Each week, expect students to review upcoming unit and come to class with questions. Prod if necessary.

_____Today starts a year-long focus on keyboarding speed, accuracy, and touch typing. Discuss why students learn keyboarding. Common Core requires "*Use [of] technology...to produce and publish writing...*"

_____Where do they use this skill? Does it transfer from school to home and life? How fast should students keyboard (Hint: fast enough to keep up with their thoughts)? Is accuracy important?

_____Today, students will evaluate both keyboarding and handwriting speed by typing and writing a document. Why measure both? By a show of hands, who thinks they type faster or handwrite faster? (Hint: most 7th graders type faster). If they handwrite faster, they probably don't like typing, and vice versa.

_____Warm up with installed software or online keyboarding program. Review posture, hand position, placement of keyboard/mouse, best practices for keyboarding.

_____At this point in student keyboarding development, they should:

> o *Keep copy to side of keyboard*
> o *Use correct posture—legs in front, body in front and one hand's width from table, elbows at sides, posture upright, feet flat on floor, hands curled over home row*
> o *Take proper care of tech equipment*
> o *Effectively use software and internet-based sites for keyboarding*

Best Practices

- *Students learn to type as fast as they need to for classwork. Set a goal of 35-45 wpm—exceeding the speed students handwrite.*
- *Focus on speed and accuracy, but remember good habits like proper hand and body position.*
- *Work on shortkeys*
- *Keep eyes off keyboard*

_____By the end of 7th grade, students should (see list at end of unit):

> o *Type 40 wpm*
> o *Type three pages in a single sitting*
> o *Compose at keyboard with ease*
> o *Keep eyes on copy*
> o *Know at least twenty shortkeys (i.e., Alt+F4, Esc, Ctrl+P, Ctrl+S, Ctrl+C, Ctrl+V, Ctrl+Alt+Del, Ctrl+B/I/U, double-click to enlarge window, Alt+Tab, Win key, Shift+tab, right mouse button key, Ctrl+, Ctrl-, ???)*
> o *Reach fingers from home row to other keys. When viewed, hands should appear still with fingers moving—no flying hands.*
> o *Touch type all keys*
> o *Understand all keys (see sample at end of Unit)*
> o *Be able to present their thoughts in written format in a way that represents student well—good formatting, minimal errors, quickly. Have they ever watched a friend labor over typing a note? What did you think about that? Have they read a typed note from someone with lots of typos? Did they ignore typos or wonder about the person's competency?*
> o *Understand keyboard parts and functions*

_____Use checklist at end of Unit to track student progress throughout year.

_____Open TypingTest.com or similar. Students select a three-minute quiz. Let them independently determine how to do this (if they haven't before).

_____As students work, walk around and observe important posture points. This is incorporated into final grade.

_____When finished, grade based on 1) wpm, 2) mistakes, and 3) observation of good keyboarding habits.

_____First quiz of year is a benchmark. Future grades are based on improvement:

- *20% improvement*   *10/10*
- *10-20% improvement*   *9/10*
- *1-10% improvement*   *8/10*
- *No improvement*   *7/10*
- *Slowed down*   *6/10*

_____Let students know Mulligan Rule applies. What's that? Any golfers? A 'mulligan' is a do-over. Students can retake any quiz/project/test covered by Mulligan Rule without losing credit. I love the Mulligan Rule. It covers all those times students complain they weren't ready, didn't know about a quiz, were sick, shouldn't be graded because [fill in the blank]. I don't argue. I smile and let them retake it. Few do. It requires little from me, yet I seem like the world's fairest teacher.

_____Next: Students handwrite pages from a book being read in class to evaluate handwriting speed. Do this for three minutes (same length as keyboarding). When done, students place word count at bottom of sheet and turn in.

_____Discuss purpose of this evaluation. What is the fastest handwriting speed? How about typing speed? If your students are like the average, most can't handwrite faster than 35ish wpm—slower than they type. What conclusion do they draw?

_____Record names of students who typed faster than they handwrote (you can use the sheet at end of Unit) and post. Add to this list as students become proficient.

_____Next: Students take a blank keyboard quiz to see what keys they know (see sample at end of Unit). This can be done in groups. Use first blank keyboard quiz as a benchmark (much like speed quiz). On subsequent ones, expect students to improve. This can be pass/fail. Students who remember all keys can be awarded a special prize (or whatever works for your student group).

_____Review important keys students should know (see end of Unit).

_____Keyboarding is a cumulative skill. What can be learned in one grade depends heavily upon what was learned earlier. If hunt 'n peck habits (or more recently, keying with thumbs) become ingrained, it's difficult to develop competence later.

_____Basics:

- *Keep hands curved over home row*
- *Use correct posture for typing*
    - *Sit straight, shoulders back, head up, body centered in front of keyboard about one hand's width from table, feet flat on ground*
    - *Keep elbows close to sides*
    - *Reach for keys—don't move hands (only fingers move)*
- *Touch type with a steady, even pace*
- *Keep copy to side of keyboard, eyes on copy or screen—NOT keyboard*

_____Seventh grade is a combination of the following typing activities:

- *Key memorization with:*
    - *Work on each row*
    - *Work on two-letter words and common phrases*
    - *One-time Brown Bear typing challenge*
- *Continuous practice with a graduated program like Type to Learn or Typing Web*
- *Covered hands during typing practice*
- *Reinforcement of shortkeys to make typing faster, easier, and more fun*
- *Anecdotal observation by teacher of typing skills*
- *Monthly finger warm-ups as a reminder that all fingers are used for keyboarding and all of them function*
- *Quarterly quizzes*
- *Quarterly keyboard challenge (see example at end of Unit)*

_____Summarize typing expectations and add each milestone to online class calendar.

_____Start **Month #1** with five minutes of finger warm-ups, Repeat once a month to show students they have ten fingers that work. Go to http://learnkeyboarding.wikispaces.com/Keyboarding+Warm-ups for fun exercises.

_____**Start class** by working on one keyboard row at a time, using Typing Lessons, Peter's Online Typing Course, or Nimble Fingers (Google for addresses).

_____Here's a schedule for the **first six weeks**:

- *Weeks 1-2: home row*
- *Weeks 3-4: QWERTY row*
- *Weeks 5-6: lower row*

_____Students practice 10-15 minutes during class and 45 minutes per week as homework.

_____**By Month #3** (after two weeks on each of three rows), students practice mastering two-letter words (http://www.nimblefingers.com/teachers.htm#checkit—scroll to bottom). This will be difficult at first, and then fun—a game. Help students stick with it through impossible to challenging to huzzah.

_____Have students take a fun 'test' to celebrate their improved keyboarding skills. Remember Brown Bear Typing—a favorite from kindergarten, first and second grades? Return to it and have a fifteen-minute contest to see who gets the highest score. This focuses solely on key placement—no worries about hand positions. Award winner something that suits your student group.

_____**Month #4,** students switch to installed software or a free online program like Typing Web. Here, they'll spend the rest of typing practice time for year. Students cover hands while practicing. I provide cloths they use at school and take home if they'd like. It feels hard at first and quickly becomes easier. The focus is on speed and accuracy.

_____As students type, anecdotally observe posture, hand position, eye placement. Make suggestions to the class when you see an endemic problem.

_____Typing is best learned in authentic projects that collaborate with classroom inquiry. No later than **Month #2**, begin project-based typing (using word processing) that integrates into classroom units. These can be short reports, magazines, trifolds, a story—pick one that works for your school.

_____**End of Unit:** Students again compare handwriting with typing speed by using both to: 1) record an already-written document (say, pages from a book they are reading), and 2) record their thoughts (say, about a book they read). Compare speed at both.

_____**Each grading period**, students take a ten-fifteen minute blank keyboard quiz (see end of unit for example) to test knowledge of key placement. They can work in pairs and must retake until they pass. This knowledge translates to speed and accuracy.

_____**Each grading period,** students take a keyboard quiz using TypingTest.com or similar. As students take quiz, anecdotally notice who is using all fingers and correct posture. Those that aren't, lose points.

Assessment Strategies

- *Quizzes*
- *Previewed material and came to class with questions*
- *Anecdotal observation*
- *Graded formative keyboard quizzes*
- *Transferred skills to class-work*
- *Summative tests*

_____**Throughout year**, observe students as they type and evaluate their errors. The cause of error is often more important than the mistake:

- *Errors such as reversals, typing an "e" instead of an "r", and omission or addition of letters are more often due to poor planning or thinking than they are to inaccurate finger placement.*
- *Other causes of errors include tension, wandering attention, faulty reading, or the wrong mind set.*
- *Watch students for fatigue—moving heads, massaging, tight facial expressions.*

_____**Throughout year**, reinforce use of shortkeys (see list at end of unit). These are quick macros for commonly-performed tasks. For example:

- *When saving, Ctrl+S*
- *When printing, Ctrl+P*
- *When needing to undo an action, Ctrl+Z*
- *When copying, Ctrl+C*
- *When pasting, Ctrl+V (why not Ctrl+P?)*
- *When enlarging a window, double click title bar*
- *When unable to close a program, Alt+F4*
- *When toggling between two windows (say, for research), Alt+Tab*
- *When entering date, Shift+Alt+D*
- *When taskbar disappears (some pesky student hid it), push Win key*
- *When indenting in a list, use Tab and Shift+tab*

_____Students love to show off their techie-ness with these.

_____Remind students to transfer knowledge to classroom or home.

_____Tuck chairs under desk, headphones over tower; leave station as it was.

_____As you teach, incorporate lesson vocabulary.

Extension:

- *Play Keyboard Challenge (see sample, end of Unit) to see who remembers what keys*
- *Students visit class internet start page for websites aligned with classwork.*
- *Homework: Students practice keyboarding to familiarize themselves with the program they will use this year (i.e., TypingWeb.com or similar). Add to class calendar.*
- *Homework: Review problem solving knowledge in preparation for next unit. Bring questions to class. Add this to class calendar.*

More Information:

- *Lesson questions? Go to http://askatechteacher.com*
- *Read "When is Typing Faster Than Handwriting?" at end of unit*
- *Follow 7th grade keyboard curriculum in K-8 Keyboard Curriculum (http://ow.ly/j6GH8)*
- *Follow Digital Citizenship Curriculum (http://www.structuredlearning.net/book/k-8-digital-citizenship-curriculum/)*

If you don't get through everything, check completed items so you know what to get back to when you have time later. I find as I focus on the central idea of a lesson, clarifying questions sometimes take more time than I'd expect. I'm fine with that.

"If a man does his best, what else is there?"

- General George S. Patton (1885-1945)

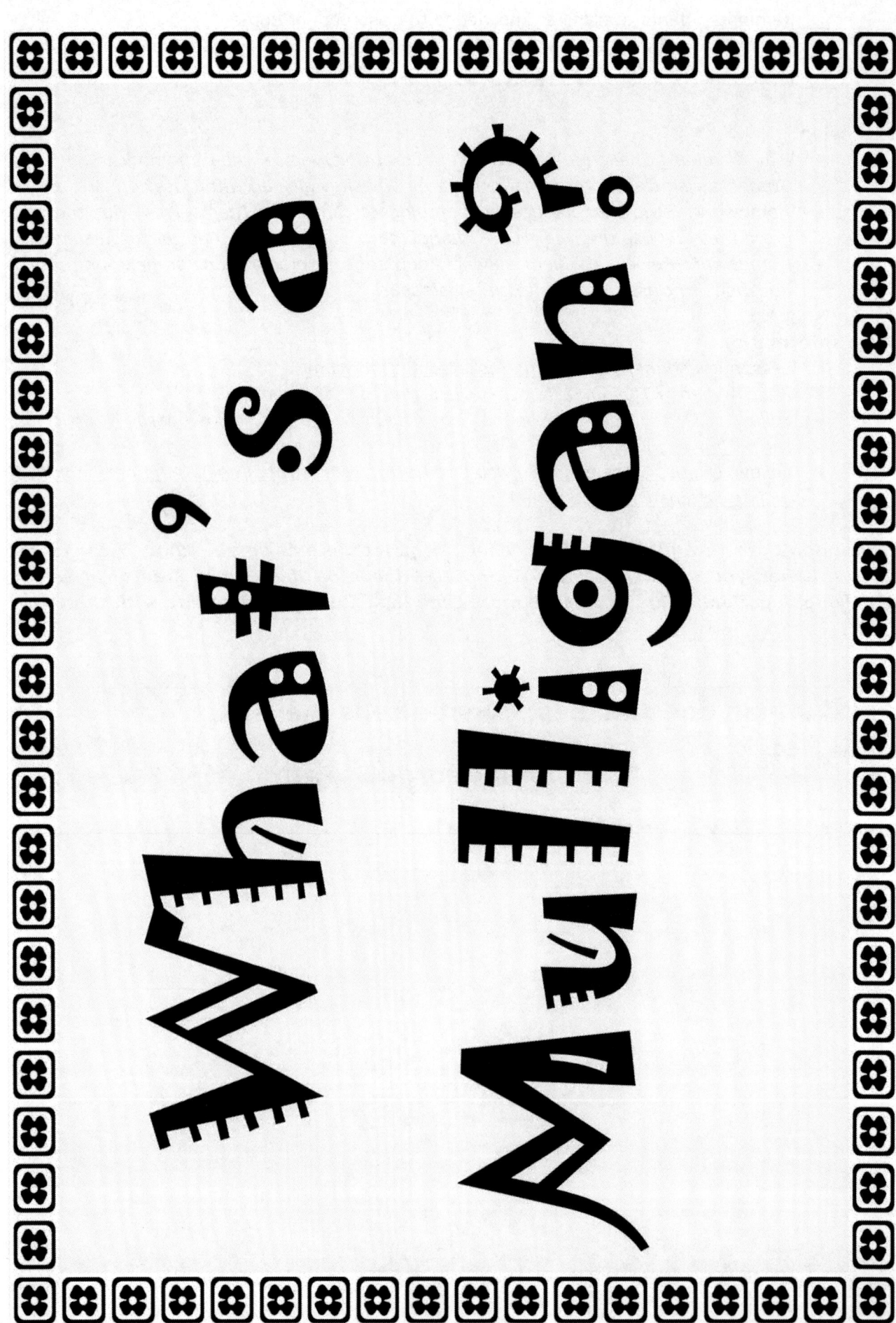

What's a Mulligan?

Who Types Faster Than They Handwrite?

Here's how fast the typical student writes by hand (from our class experiment):

(enter your class speed)

Here are seventh graders who type faster:

1. _____

2. _____

3. _____

4. _____

5. _____

6. _____

7. _____

8. _____

9. _____

10. _____

Blank Keyboard

Name: _____

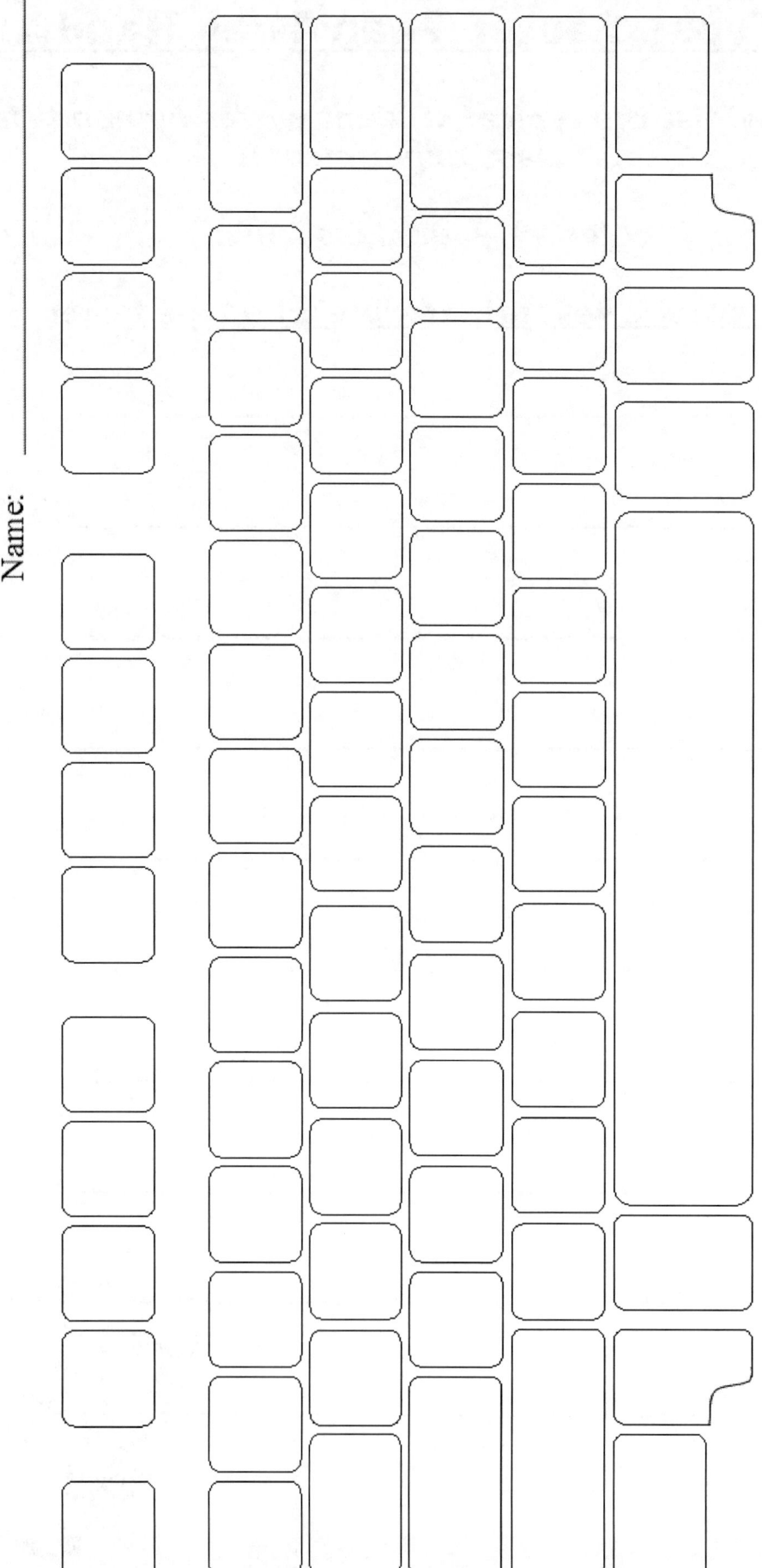

Shortkeys

	Problem	Solution
1	Today's date	Shift+Alt+D
2.	Current Time	Shift+Alt+T
3.	Exit a program	Alt+F4
4.	Double click doesn't work	Push enter
5.	Start button disappeared	Windows button on keyboard
6.	Erased my document	Ctrl+Z
7.	Menu command is grey	Press escape 4 times and try again
8.	Need task manager	Ctrl+Alt+Del
9.	Copy	Ctrl+C
10.	Print	Ctrl+P
11.	Need to toggle between 2 programs?	Alt+Tab
12.	Can't find a program?	Use Search function on Start

15 Critical Keys to Know

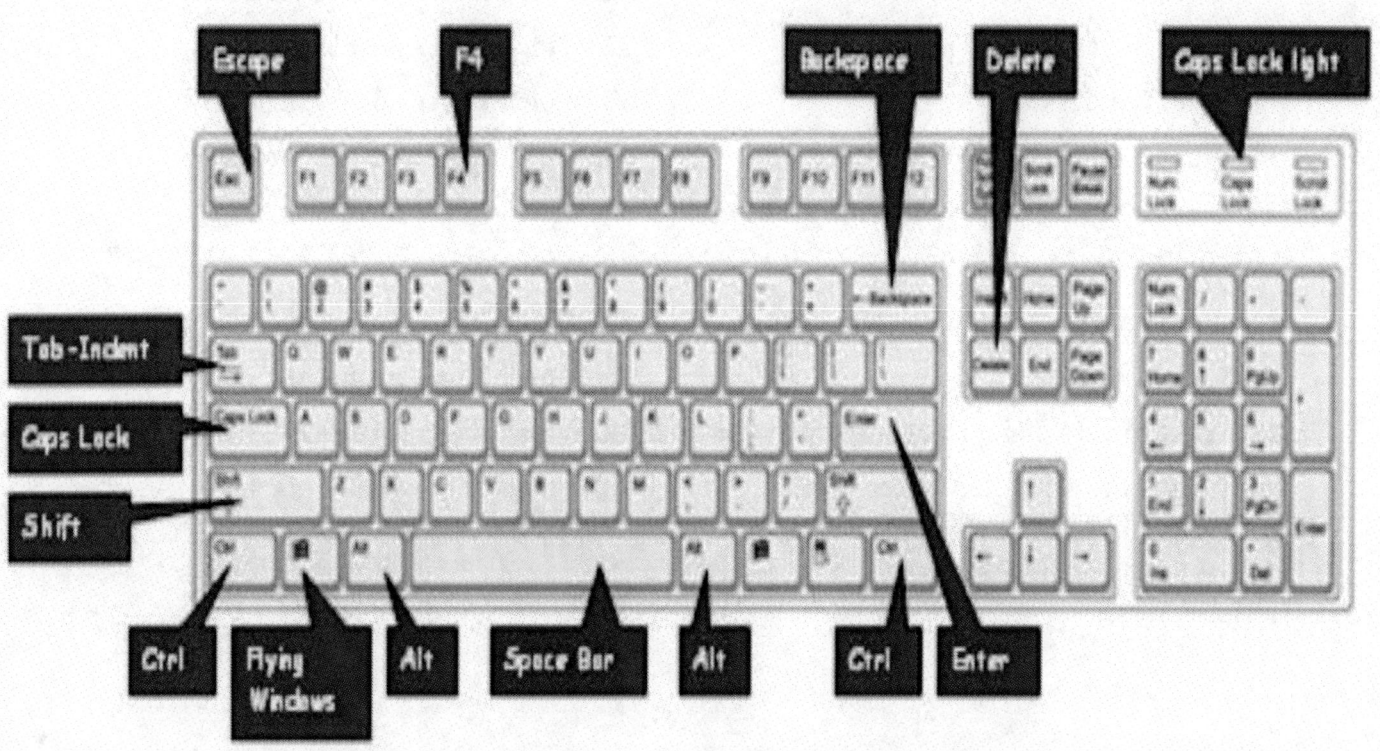

KEYBOARD CHALLENGE
Review
Review the following concepts. These are similar to questions that will be asked during the Team Keyboard Challenge to find the most tech-savvy student!

1. Do you have cat claws or dog paws at computer? Why?
2. How do you capitalize a letter
3. How do you find f and j without looking
4. In general, do fingers or hands move in finding keys
5. In general, which finger pushes a key
6. Name one key your right thumb pushes
7. Name three keys middle finger pushes
8. Name three keys pinkie pushes
9. Name three keys you use pointer to push
10. Name three keys ring finger pushes
11. What are three rules on how you sit at keyboard
12. What finger pushes enter
13. What is a desktop
14. What is one keyboard shortcut
15. What is typing without looking at keys called
16. What part of chair do you sit on when keyboarding
17. What row do finger start on while typing
18. What's the computer log in
19. What's the computer password
20. What shortkey exits a program
21. What's the row above home row
22. What's the row below home row
23. What's your password for TTL4
24. Where are elbows when keyboarding
25. Where does right thumb rest when keyboarding
26. Which finger do you use for enter
27. Which finger do you use for escape
28. Which finger do you use for shift
29. Which finger do you use for backspace
30. Which finger pushes the a key
31. Which finger pushes the ac key
32. Which finger pushes the b key
33. Which finger pushes the d key
34. Which finger pushes the e key
35. Which finger pushes the f key
36. Which finger pushes the g key
37. Which finger pushes the h key
38. Which finger pushes the i key
39. Which finger pushes the j key
40. Which finger pushes the k key

KEYBOARDING SCOPE AND SEQUENCE CHECKLIST

Posture

_____*Copy to the side of keyboard*
_____*Correct posture—legs in front, body in front, elbows at sides*
_____*Hands curled over home row (not flat)*
_____*Feet flat on the floor*
_____*Keyboard one inch off edge of table*
_____*Sit straight, body centered one hand's width from table*

Keyboarding

_____*Types 40 wpm by end of 7th grade*
_____*Types three pages in a single sitting by end of 7th grade*
_____*Compose at keyboard with ease*
_____*Demonstrate proper care and handling of keyboard*
_____*Effectively use internet-based sites for keyboarding*
_____*Effectively use lab software for keyboarding*
_____*Keep eyes on copy most of the time*
_____*Key paragraphs with enter and tab*
_____*Learn twenty basic keyboard shortcuts (Alt+F4, Esc, Ctrl+P, Ctrl+S, Ctrl+C, Ctrl+V, Ctrl+Alt+Del, Ctrl+B/I/U, double-click to enlarge window, Alt+Tab, Win key, Shift+tab, right mouse button key, Ctrl+ (to zoom in), Ctrl- (to zoom out), ???)*
_____*Rest fingers on home row, reach for other keys. When viewed, hands should appear still with fingers moving—no flying hands.*
_____*Set keyboard goal for students (wpm and pages typed per seating)*
_____*Touch type all keys*
_____*Touch type many two- and three- letter words and phrases with speed and accuracy*
_____*Understand all keyboard keys*
_____*Understand difference between backspace, delete*
_____*Understand use of arrow keys*

When is Typing Faster Than Handwriting?

Most elementary-age students struggle with typing. This doesn't surprise me. They've been handwriting since kindergarten. They're proud of their new cursive skills. It's easy to grab and pencil and write. Typing, though requires setting up their posture, hand position, trying to remember where all those pesky keys are (why aren't they just alphabetized? It's a good point. Discuss that with students).

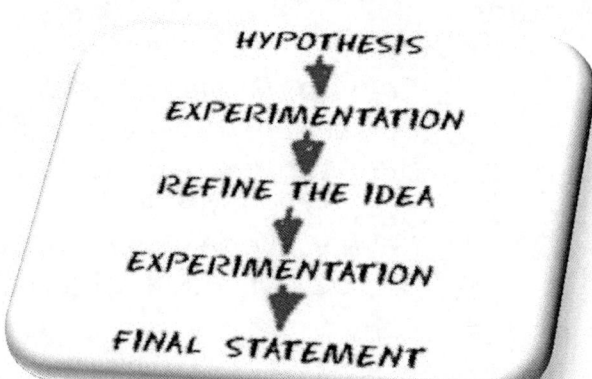

In third grade, I gather the students and we chat about it. Why do they have to learn to keyboard? It's more than a skill they trot out for the keyboarding software and then forget. Discuss the idea of sharing ideas–the Gutenberg Press, when writing began with scrolls and rocks, why was it important to save ideas in perpetuity? Why is it important to students?

The discussion should come around to the idea that putting ideas in some sort of permanent fashion is important to the history of mankind. The question is how, and the 'how' that's relevant to the students is a comparison of handwriting and keyboarding. Here's where we go from there:

Circle back on science in technology

- Discuss whether students handwrite faster/slower than they type. Ask students to share thoughts on why their opinion is true. You are likely to get opinions on both sides of this discussion. If not, prod students with logic for both.
- When it's clear the class is divided on this subject (or not–that's fine too), suggest running an experiment to see which is faster—handwriting or typing.
- Circle back to science class and engage in a discussion on the Scientific Method. Develop a hypothesis for this class research, something like: *Third grade students in Mr. X's class can handwrite faster than they type* (this is the most common opinion in my classes).
- Have students hand-copy the typing quiz they took earlier in the trimester for 3 minutes.
- Analyze the results: Compare their handwriting speed to their typing speed. I encourage an individual comparison as well as a class average comparison to help with understanding the conclusion.
- Discuss results: Why do students think some students typed faster and others typed slower? (In my classes, third graders typed approx. 10 wpm and handwrote approx. 15 wpm. Discussion was heated and enthusiastic on reasons. Especially valuable were the thoughts of those rare students who typed faster).
- Students will offer lots of reasons for slower typing (they're new to typing, don't do it much in class, their hands got off on the keyboard). In truth, the logistics of typing make it the hands-

down winner once key placement is secured. Fingers on a keyboard are significantly faster than the moving pencil.

- One reason students suggest is that they don't usually type from copy. Key in on this reason (quite valid, I think—don't you?) and revise the experiment to have students type and handwrite from a prompt.
- What is the final conclusion?
- If possible, share results from 4-8th. What grade level do students consistently type faster than they handwrite? Why? Are students surprised by the answer?
- Post a list on the wall of students who type faster than they handwrite. This surprises everyone.

I do this experiment in 3rd, 4th and 5th grade. Third, students on average handwrite faster. By 4th, the average is the same–students can type as fast as they handwrite. This surprises them and energizes them to work harder on their keyboarding. By 5th, most students type faster, though many didn't expect that.

After this experiment, I see more students selecting keyboarding over handwriting, especially if an iPad is available rather than the cumbersome laptop or desktop. I also see them caring more about the skill of keyboarding as they realize it is their future. This has become an important tool in my keyboarding toolkit that is fully as effective as practicing drills.

For more tricks like this, check out ***The Essential Guide to Keyboarding in 45 Minutes a Week***.

Note: There are lots of examples of the scientific method and they all vary when talking about elementary grades. Talk to your science teacher and adapt this experiment to the one she uses.

Unit 4—Problem Solving

Vocabulary	Problem solving	Big Idea
• *Compare/contrast* • *Evidence* • *Failure* • *Gamification* • *Life skill* • *Logical thinking* • *Pattern* • *Problem solving* • *Proportional reasoning* • *Shortkeys* • *Strategies* • *Troubleshoot*	• *I don't know answer (Did you use all resources?)* • *I don't care about shortkeys (they are another solution to a problem)* • *I'm frustrated (but it feels great to solve a problem)* • *I can't do it (take a deep breath; try again)* • *Student computers don't work? Help solve problems—don't do for them* • *Students afraid to fail? Remind them success is based on effort, not crossing a finish line*	*Make things as simple as possible, but not simpler (Albert Einstein)*
Time Required *90 minutes*	**NETS-S Standards** *3a, 4c, 6c*	**CCSS** *CCSS.Math.Practice.M*

Essential Question
How does technology help problem solving and logical thinking?

Overview

Materials

Problem Solving board sign-up materials, Sign up genius account (if using this)

Teacher Preparation
- Talk with teachers about problem solving and thinking skills expectations
- Have Problem-Solving Board sign-up sheets on wall or online
- Ensure that all required links are on lab computer
- Have notes online for students to preview upcoming unit

Steps

_____Required skill level for this unit: No specific skills required. But: Enthusiasm for thinking expected.

_____Any questions from review of Problem Solving Unit? Expect students to come to class with questions on upcoming unit.

_____Any questions from keyboard homework?

_____Review results of keyboarding quiz. What's the average speed? What were common problems (flying fingers, hunt-and-peck, eyes on hands)? Who were 'speedsters'?

_____Introduce Problem Solving. This is a life skill that transcends a subject. Expect students to transfer knowledge to all parts of life.

_____Discuss quote under 'Big Idea'. Who said that? What's it mean? Discuss quotes at end of unit. Take ten minutes for students to blog about one.

_____Discuss what it means to be a 'problem solver'. Who do students go to when they need a problem solved? Parents? Do students believe that person gets it right more often than others? Would they believe most people are wrong half the time?

_____Problem solving is closely aligned with logical thinking, critical thinking, reasoning, and thought habits. Discuss why students should become problem solvers (hint: refer to prior point—most people students go to for assistance are wrong half the time). Discuss characteristics of a 'problem solver':

- *Use appropriate tools strategically (from Common Core)*
- *Attend to precision (from Common Core)*
- *Make sense of problems and persevere in solving them (from Common Core)*
- *Value evidence (from Common Core)*
- *Comprehend as well as critique (from Common Core)*
- *Understand other perspectives and cultures (from Common Core)*
- *Demonstrate independence (from Common Core)*

_____Additionally, they can:

- *Identify and define authentic problems/questions for investigation*
- *Accept responsibility for solving their own problems*
- *Troubleshoot a non-working program*
- *Learn new tech skills by reflecting on past knowledge*
- *Know which program is right for what task*

_____Finally, being as problem solver:

- *Is fundamental to an educated person*
- *Is required of a responsible citizenship in a democratic society*
- *Is critical for a wide range of jobs*

_____Background:

- Robinson states in her 1987 practicum report:
  Teaching children to become effective thinkers is increasingly recognized as an immediate goal of education....If students are to function successfully in a highly technical society, then they must be equipped with lifelong learning and thinking skills necessary to acquire and process information in an ever-changing world (p. 16)."Teaching Thinking Skills"
- Beyth-Marom, et al. characterize thinking as making good choices:

  Thinking skills are necessary tools in a society characterized by rapid change, many alternatives of actions, and numerous individual and collective choices and decisions. —("Enhancing Children's Thinking Skills: An Instructional Model for Decision-Making Under Certainty." INSTRUCTIONAL SCIENCE 16/3 1987)

_____Discuss strategies students use for problem solving:

- *Use tools available to solve a problem*
- *Observe and collect data*
- *Be aware of surroundings*

- o Notice the forest and the trees
- o Try to solve problems before asking for help
- o Think logically
- o Never saying 'can't'
- o Act out a problem situation
- o Apply inductive reasoning
- o Break a problem into simpler parts
- o Distinguish between relevant and irrelevant information
- o Draw a diagram
- o Guess and check
- o See patterns
- o Translate data into mathematical language.
- o Try, fail, try again
- o Use conjecture and evidence to develop valid rules and procedures.
- o Use proportional reasoning
- o Use what has worked in the past
- o Work backwards

Best Practices

- Teachers are guides
- Embrace change
- Question 'the way it's always been done'
- Be aware of your surroundings
- Use available tools to solve problems
- Identify authentic problems, ask clarifying questions, trust yourself
- Do not fear being a risk-taker
- Let solutions be inquiry-driven

_____Two major projects will demonstrate problem solving:

- o Teach classmates to use a program
- o Self-teach and use a program in a project

_____Discuss Problem Solving Board—starts next week (see next pages). Add start date to class online calendar. It covers issues students face when they use technology. (Note: As you move through the year, keep a list of problems for next year's Board.)

_____Board presentation requires 1) independent investigation, 2) risk-taking for cautious students who feel a Right Answer lives out there somewhere, and 3) presentation skills discussed in Common Core under 'Speaking and Listening':

- Come prepared, having researched material.
- Present findings, emphasizing points in a focused, coherent manner with pertinent descriptions, facts, details, examples.
- Use appropriate eye contact, adequate volume, and clear pronunciation.
- Adapt speech to the context and task.

_____Students sign up via a program like Sign up Genius or Google Apps. If neither is available, use wall posters (see end of unit):

- Select a presentation date.
- Select a problem to teach classmates.
- Get solution from family, friends, or even teacher as a last resort.
- Teach classmates how to solve problem.

- *Take questions.*

_____Entire presentation takes about three minutes.

_____Review grading (see next pages).

_____Discuss most common problems students face when using tech (see list at end of unit). Students should own these by end of class.

_____Remind students to transfer knowledge to classroom or home.

_____Tuck chairs under desk, headphones over tower; leave station as it was.

_____As you teach, incorporate lesson vocabulary.

Extension:

- *Students add their presentation date to class calendar if possible.*
- *Homework: Review word processing (i.e., Word) in preparation for next week's assessment.*
- *Add word processing assessment to class online calendar.*

More Information:

- *Read "The Secret to Teaching Tech: Delegate" at end of unit*
- *New teacher? Read "5 Must-have Skills for New Tech Teachers" at end of unit*
- *Questions? Go to http://askatechteacher.com*
- *Follow keyboard lessons in K-8 Keyboard Curriculum (http://ow.ly/j6GH8)*
- *Follow Digital Citizenship Curriculum (http://www.structuredlearning.net/book/k-8-digital-citizenship-curriculum/)*

If you don't get through everything, check completed items so you know what to get back to when you have time later. I find as I focus on the central idea of a lesson, clarifying questions sometimes take more time than I'd expect. I'm fine with that.

"The measure of success is not whether you have a tough problem to deal with, but whether it is the same problem you had last year."

— John Foster Dulles *Former Secretary of State*

Problem Solving Board Sign-up

	Class #1	Class #2	Class #3
Week of _____			
Week of _____			
Week of _____			
Week of _____			
Week of _____			
Week of _____			
Week of _____			
Week of _____			

Sample Problems	Class #1	Class #2	Class #3
When do I save and when 'save as'			
What if the monitor doesn't work			
What if the volume doesn't work			
What if the computer doesn't work			
What if the mouse doesn't work			
When do I backspace and when delete			
What are 5 useful shortkeys			
What's 'see the forest for the trees'			
What does 'select-do' mean			
I can't find a tool I need			
What if my toolbar disappears			
What if the document disappears			
My doc is too large to email			
How do I search for a file			
How do I rename a folder			
What if the program freezes			
What's a Mulligan? In this class?			
My internet toolbar disappeared			
What does 'BCC' mean in an email			
How do I exit a screen I'm stuck in			
How do I use Discussion in the wiki			
I don't have Word at home. What do I do			
My file's 'read only'. What do I do			
How do I make a macro in Word			
What's the difference between format-edit			
How do I add a hyperlink in Word			
Why use Word? Why use Excel? PowerPoint?			
How do I embed a widget			
How do I save a blog post			
How do I edit a Google Earth placemark			
What are three ways to communicate something			
Is it better to communicate with words or images			
What is brainstorming? Mind mapping?			
How do I protect my digital footprint			
3 ways to keep my info private on the internet			
How do I share/collaborate on Google Apps			
What are 3 digital rights? Responsibilities			
When must I use proper grammar on internet			

PROBLEM SOLVING BOARD
Grading Rubric

Name: _____

Knew question   _____

Knew answer   _____

Asked audience for help if didn't know answer   _____

No umm's, stutters   _____

No nervous movements (giggles, wiggles, etc.)   _____

Overall   _____

PROBLEM SOLVING BOARD
Grading Rubric

Name: _____

Knew question   _____

Knew answer   _____

Asked audience for help if didn't know answer   _____

No umm's, stutters   _____

No nervous movements (giggles, wiggles, etc.)   _____

Overall   _____

Common problems students face with computers

	Problem	Solution
1.	My browser is too small	Double click blue bar
2.	Browser tool bar missing	Push F11
3.	Can't exit a program	Alt+F4
4.	What's today's date	Hover over clock Shift+Alt+D in Word
5.	Double click doesn't work	Push enter
7.	Start button disappeared	Use Windows button
8.	Program disappeared	Check taskbar
9.	Erased my document	Ctrl+Z
10.	I can't find a tool	Right click on screen; it'll show most common tools
11.	My screen is frozen	Clear a dialogue box Press Escape four times
12.	My menu command is grey	Press escape 4 times and try again
13.	Can't find Bold, Italic, Underline	Use Ctrl+B, Ctrl+I, Ctrl+U
14.	Can't find the program	Push Start, use 'Search' field
15.	Internet toolbar's gone	Push F11
16.	My computer doesn't work	Check monitor/tower power, plugs
17.	My programs are gone	Are you logged in correctly?

USE KEYBOARD SHORTCUTS. GET DONE FASTER

Great Quotes About Problem Solving

"In times like these it is good to remember that there have always been times like these."
— Paul Harvey *Broadcaster*

"Never try to solve all the problems at once — make them line up for you one-by-one."
— Richard Sloma

"Some problems are so complex that you have to be highly intelligent and well-informed just to be undecided about them."
— Laurence J. Peter

"Life is a crisis - so what!"
— Malcolm Bradbury

"You don't drown by falling in the water; you drown by staying there."
— Edwin Louis Cole

"The significant problems we face cannot be solved at the same level of thinking we were at when we created them."
— Albert Einstein

"It is not stress that kills us. It is effective adaptation to stress that allows us to live."
— George Vaillant

"The most serious mistakes are not being made as a result of wrong answers. The truly dangerous thing is asking the wrong questions."
— Peter Drucker *Men, Ideas & Politics*

"The problem is not that there are problems. The problem is expecting otherwise and thinking that having problems is a problem."
— Theodore Rubin

It's not that I'm so smart, it's just that I stay with problems longer.
—Albert Einstein

No problem can stand the assault of sustained thinking.
—Voltaire

The problem is not that there are problems. The problem is expecting otherwise and thinking that having problems is a problem.
—Theodore Rubin

Problems are only opportunities with thorns on them.
—Hugh Miller

The Secret to Teaching Tech: Delegate

There's a secret to teaching kids how to use technology. It's called 'delegate'. I don't mean sluff off the teaching to aides or parents. Here, I'm referring to empowering students to be their own problem-solvers, then expect it of them. Here's how you do it:

- Let them know technology isn't difficult. Aw, come on. I see your scrunched faces. Here's the ugly little truth: Technology is only hard to learn if kids are *told* it's hard to learn. Don't mention it. Compare keyboarding to piano—a skill lots of kids feel good about—or another one that relates to your particular group. Remove the fear. They might not believe you, but you're the teacher so they'll give you a chance

- Teach them how to do the twenty most common problems they'll face on a computer (more on that later). Expect them to know these—do pop quizzes if that's your teaching style). Post them on the walls. Do a Problem-solving Board (click the link for details on that—it works well in my classes). Remind them if they know these, they'll have 70% less problems (that's true, too) than the kids who don't know how to solve these. If they raise their hand and ask for help, play Socrates and force them to think through the answer. Sometimes I point to the wall. Sometimes I ask the class for help (without saying who needs assistance. Embarrassing students is counter-productive). Pick the way that works for you. The only solution you *can't* employ is to do it for them

- Teach students keyboard shortcuts. Does that sound like an odd suggestion? It isn't. Students learn in different ways. Some are best with menus, ribbons and mouse clicks. Some like the easy and speed of the keyboard. Give them that choice. If they know both ways, they'll pick the one that works best for them. Once they know these, they'll be twice as likely to remember one of the two methods of doing the skill like exit a program (Alt+F4) or print (Ctrl+P).

- Let neighbors help neighbors. I resisted this for several years, thinking they'd end up chatting about other topics than tech. They don't when sufficiently motivated and interested. They are excited to show off their knowledge by helping classmates.

5 Must-have Skills for New Tech Teachers

If you teach technology, it's likely you were thrown into it by your Admin. You used to be a first grade teacher or the science expert or maybe even the librarian and suddenly, you walked into school one day and found out you'd become that tech person down the hall you were always in awe of, the one responsible for classroom computers, programs, curriculum, and everything in between. Now that's you—the go-to person for tech problems, computer quirks, crashes and freezes, and tech tie-ins for classroom inquiry.

You have no idea where to begin.

Here's a peek into your future: On that first propitious day, everything will change. Your colleagues will assume you received a data upload of the answers to every techie question. It doesn't matter that yesterday, you were one of them. Now, you will be on a pedestal, colleague's necks craned upward as they ask , *How do I get the SmartScreen to work?* or *We need microphones for a lesson I'm starting in three minutes. Can you please-please-please fix them?* You will nod your head, smile woodenly, and race to your classroom for the digital manuals (if you're lucky) or Google for online help.

Let me start by saying: Don't worry. Really. You'll learn by doing, just as we teach students. Take a deep breath, engage your brain, and let your brilliance shine.

That's the number one skill—confidence—but there are a five other practical strategies that have worked for those who came before you. Consider:

Be a communicator

Talk to grade-level teachers weekly. Scaffold your lessons with what they teach. Ask them to stay during tech class and offer on-the-spot tie-ins between what you teach and they say in class. Yes, they might want/need the time for planning or meetings, but the benefit to students of this team-teaching approach is tremendous. And it benefits the teachers, also. Many of them are not yet sold on integrating tech into their classrooms. They know they must if they're in one of the 46 Common Core adoptive states, but they don't like it, don't know how to do it, and don't see why it's so important. When they see you do it, they will be more willing to weave it into their lessons. For example, when they hear how you reinforce good keyboarding skills, they will be more likely to insist on those traits in their classroom.

Be a risk-taker

Flaunt your cheeky geekiness. Start a Twitter feed. Use your iPhone as a timer for a speed test or the iPad to scan in an art project for a digital portfolio. At any opportunity, share your geek glee with students. Let them see that tech is part of life, not a subject taught in school. It's a habit, a time-saver, a facilitator, a joy. It won't take long to convert them. A couple of admiring glances from friends or appreciative thanks from parents and they'll be sold.

Be an explorer

Go to the grade-level classrooms and demonstrate how technology is part of learning. This can be via iPads, the class pod of computers, the netbooks, or whatever is available. Ask students what they are doing in class and offer tech methods to make it easier. For example, are they submitting homework in a pile on the teacher's desk? Try a drop box—or email. Could they type reports instead of handwrite them (I know—this gets philosophic, so be prepared for that discussion)? Instead of hand-drawn posters where success leans toward the artistically-talented, could they use Glogster? Encourage students to plug in during class.

Be a negotiator

You need parental buy-in on tech ed, but it is a topic typically outside their comfort zone. I often hear from 2nd grade parents that their children know more than they do (I'm talking MS Office, internet use, and some online tools). Understand that this frightens them and part of your job is to mitigate their fears. Here are some ideas:

- Have your door always open. Be ready and willing to talk with them about how to complete their child's projects—not so they can do for them, but so they feel it is within their child's grasp. Take as long as needed and welcome them to return.
- Answer parent tech questions, even if it's about a home computer problem. My experience is these are often simple, but intimidating. If you mitigate fear, you maximize support for tech ed.
- Offer a parent class that teaches the skills students are learning. Listen to your group. What makes these intelligent adults nervous about tech? Solve it for them. I often start with an agenda and end with a free-for-all, where I answer questions or help parents create fliers for soccer teams or solve home-based tech problems. It's all good. They leave feeling I'm a partner.

Don't take life too seriously

Have a sense of humor about everything. You're going to have computer meltdowns. It's why robots can't replace teachers, so embrace chaos. One of the true joys of tech is the puzzling. Why doesn't the mouse work? Why does a website work on one computer and not another? Where'd the taskbar go? Let students see how much fun it is to engage the brain.

That's it, just five skills. Any questions? Email me at askatechteacher@gmail.com.

Unit 5—Word Processing Assessment

Vocabulary	Problem solving	Big Idea
• *Alignment* • *Autoshape* • *Bullets* • *Call-out* • *Ctrl+S* • *Drop box* • *Discussion Board* • *Edit* • *Font* • *Format* • *Google Docs* • *QWERTY* • *Save early save often* • *Text (program)* • *Text box* • *TNR 12* • *Touch typing* • *Word processing*	• *Cap doesn't work (Caps lock on?)* • *Not enough time? (Word processing must be automatic. Don't feel guilty only fifteen minutes is allotted for project. That's part of assessment.* • *Can't find program? Use 'search' on Start button.* • *How do I exit a program (Alt+F4)* • *I can't find Word (use Search)* • *Got out of bullets (backspace until up against last bullet; push enter)* • *No Word (use Google Docs, Open Office, other word processor)* • *I lost my document (did you save early save often?)* • *I didn't finish the assessment (part of assessment is the time limit—can students work fast)*	*Learn and understand word processing basics*
Time Required 90 minutes	**NETS-S Standards** 2b, 6a	**CCSS** *CCSS.ELA-Literacy.W.7.6*

Essential Question
What are essential skills in word processing?

Overview

Materials

Internet, Problem Solving Board rubrics and schedule, word processing program

Teacher Preparation

- Talk with other teachers so you tie the final word processing project into their inquiry
- Have Problem-Solving Board schedule and rubrics available
- Have word processing assessment available
- Know what word processing skills students need help on (based on assessment) for second class
- Have notes online for students to preview upcoming unit

Steps

_____**Required skill level: familiarity with word processing, particularly program used at school.** Students who have used the SL curriculum since 2nd grade will be ready. Others: Adapt expectations.

_____Any questions on keyboard homework? Use <u>Nimble Fingers,</u> Typing Web or similar

(Google for website) on home row or QWERTY row (whichever students have reached by this point in the school year).

_____Any questions from homework (word processing review)? Expect students to have reviewed upcoming unit and brought questions to class.

_____Start Problem Solving Board. All students should be signed up for a problem and presentation date. Students can get solution from family, friends, neighbors or even teacher as a last resort. They will teach classmates how to solve the problem.

_____Before starting assessment, what is 'word processing'? Name some word processing programs (Hint: Word, Word Perfect, Google Docs, Open Office, Text). Why is it important to be able to use them:

- *Communicate information and ideas effectively to multiple audiences with a variety of media and formats.*
- *Understand how email/forums/blogs help students communicate and collaborate (are these word processing?).*
- *Know what tasks are best suited to word processing as opposed to presentation programs or spreadsheets.*
- *Produce/publish writing and present relationships between information and ideas clearly and efficiently (from Common Core).*
- *Integrate information from different media to develop a coherent understanding of a topic or issue (from Common Core).*
- *Write routinely for a range of discipline-specific tasks, purposes, and audiences (from Common Core).*

_____Display word processing assessment on class SmartScreen or provide copies in read-only format that students bring up at their stations. The samples here are in Word, but you can use Google Docs, Open Office, or other by adapting assessment to those programs. Allocate balance of class to complete assessment. Students must work independently.

_____Walk around to answer questions that aren't skills related.

_____Remind students to 'save early save often' during quiz, about every ten minutes

_____When students are done, submit via email or dropbox (or what works for your school).

_____Have websites on class start page that tie into inquiry for those who finish early.

_____Use rubric on next pages to determine skills class requires assistance with.

_____Second class: Review difficult skills both by demonstrating and by student doing.

_____Finish unit by using all word processing program skills in a project for one of their classes—a literature review, historic analysis, science discussion.

_____As you teach, use correct vocabulary.

_____Throughout class, check for understanding. And, expect students to solve problems/make decisions.

_____Remind students to transfer knowledge to classroom or home.

_____Tuck chairs under desk, headphones over tower; leave station as it was.

Extension:
- *Have students blog (if available) on difficulties/ease of this assessment and final project. If no student blogs, set up a Discussion Board. This can be done as homework.*
- *Have students prepare for and take the* <u>*MS Word certification*</u>.
- *Homework: Review Excel in preparation for assessment.*
- *Add Excel Assessment to online class calendar.*

More Information:
- *See article at end of Unit, "7 More Word Best Practices"*
- *Unit questions? Go to* <u>*http://askatechteacher.com*</u>

If you don't get through everything, check completed items so you know what to get back to when you have time later. I find as I focus on the central idea of a lesson, clarifying questions sometimes take more time than I'd expect. I'm fine with that.

> **"The artist is nothing without the gift, but the gift is nothing without work."**
>
> **- Emile Zola (1840-1902)**

WORD ASSESSMENT

Follow the instructions below. Assessment includes how well you read and complete directions and that you finish in allotted time. Do your best. If you don't remember how to do a skill, go to next.

- Put heading on page
- Right-align heading
- Put a title underneath heading——"Word Assessment"
- Center title, font Comic Sans, font size 14, bold
- Type two paragraphs about yourself, font size 12, Times New Roman
- Change second paragraph to font size 16 and Papyrus
- Add bullets with
  1. Favorite class
  2. What you like to read
  3. Who you spend time with
- Add "The End" as WordArt at page bottom
- Add a border

> *Wherever you are, be there until you leave.*
>
> *—Anonymous*

- Add a picture
- Have text wrap around the clipart
- Put a call-out aimed at the picture
- Add an autoshape
- Color autoshape pink or red

This is easy!!!

- Add text box with what your favorite quote
- Shade text box
- Add a table with seven columns and three times during the day
- Add information for each day and each time of day
- Add footer with student name and class

Sunday	Monday	Tuesday	Wednesday	Thursday	Friday	Saturday
Ate breakfast						
Ate lunch						
Ate dinner						

The End

Grading Sheet for Word Assessment

WORD ASSESSMENT

Question		1	2	3	4	5	6	7	8	9	10	11	12	13	14	15	16	17	18	19	20
1	heading																				
	all parts																				
2	right align																				
3	title																				
	underneath																				
4	center																				
	Comic sans																				
	size 14																				
	bold																				
5	2 paragraphs																				
	size 12																				
	TNR																				
6	Para. 2																				
	size 16																				
	Papyrus																				
7	bullets																				
	daily activities																				
	ate																				
	played w/																				
8	The End																				
	Wordart																				
	page bottom																				
9	border																				
10	picture																				
11	text wrap																				
12	call-out																				
	location																				
13	autoshape																				
14	pink																				
15	footer																				
16	text box																				
	mom's words																				
17	shade text box																				
18	table																				
	7 columns																				
	3 rows																				
	heading row																				
19	table into																				
	Total	0	0	0	0	0	0	0	0	0	0	0	0	0	0	0	0	0	0	0	0

7 More Word Best Practices

The faster you teach students to be problem solvers, the more they'll learn. Computers are a foreign language. Even with small class sizes, the more students can do for themselves, the more fun they'll have learning the intricacies of technology.

The good news is, students love to be independent. They find it cool to know keyboard shortcuts for getting stuff done. In my class, students can help their neighbors, and they love showing off their problem solving skills. Here are 9 tricks that cover many common problems students will face using MS Word:

1. **Ctrl+Z–undo**
   This will be your favorite. There are too many times to mention when I've had a frantic student, almost in tears because s/he thought s/he'd lost his/her document, and two seconds later I retrieved it. I was a hero for a class period.

2. **Macro for a heading**
   This is great for students who have to remember MLA rules. What goes in a heading? How big are the margins? Where's a page number go? No worries. Create a macro and save resulting document as a template. Never again worry.

3. **How to find lost documents**
   It takes a while for users to get accustomed to saving files on a network. Often, documents end up lost (in my school, students must drill down through five levels to get to their unique location). My students learn early to use 'search' on the start menu.

4. **How to insert data**
   If students complain they lose data as they type, this is probably why. Show how to push 'insert' key and all will be fixed.

5. **Show-hide tool.**
   Kids try to strong-arm Word into doing their will–often the wrong way. My favorite is 'enter enter' as a shortcut to double space. It seems to work until they have to edit the document, and then everything gets messed up. Have students push the **show-hide button** to see if they're using the double space tool. Then, show them where the icon is.

6. **Tables—they work so much better than columns and tabs.**
   Teach it to kids **early and use it often**. It will save you miles of distress.

7. **How to insert the date**
   It takes a long time for students to remember the date. When they ask, show them **Shift+Alt+D** shortkey to insert current date into Word. They love it and it saves a lot of time for you.

Unit 6—Spreadsheet Assessment

Vocabulary	Problem solving	Big Idea
• *Average* • *Calculation* • *Count* • *Doc* • *Excel* • *Formula* • *Model* • *Precision* • *Quantitative* • *Read only* • *Spreadsheet* • *Structure* • *Workbook* • *Worksheet*	• *Can't save assessment—says 'read only' (save under a different name)* • *What's the difference between save and save-as?* • *What is today's date? (Ctrl+;)* • *Can't find doc file (Start-search)* • *Right-click doesn't work (reboot)* • *What's the 'Mulligan Rule' (do-over for quizzes/classwork)* • *Chart embeds into worksheet (highlight data; click F11)* • *How do I merge two workbooks (copy worksheet from one to other)* • *Formula won't work (did you start with =? Did you try Help?)*	***Students use spreadsheets to construct viable arguments, make sense of problems, and persevere in solving them***
Time Required *90 minutes*	**NETS-S Standards** *2b, 6a*	***CCSS*** *CCSS.Math.Content.7—intro*

Essential Question
How do I turn data into information?

Overview

Materials

Excel (or other spreadsheet program), Problem Solving rubric, inquiry websites

Teacher Preparation

- Have Problem-Solving Board rubrics
- Have assessment sheet for Excel quiz
- Determine Excel skills students need help with
- Add Google Earth summative to class online calendar
- Have notes online for students to preview upcoming unit

Steps

_____**Required skill level for this unit: introductory Excel.** Students who have used the SL curriculum since 2nd grade are ready. Others: Adapt expectations and/or teaching.

_____Continue Problem Solving Board.

_____Any questions on keyboard homework? Use <u>Nimble Fingers,</u> Typing Web or similar (Google for website) on home row or QWERTY row (whichever you are up to).

_____Any questions from Excel homework? Expect students to review upcoming unit and come to class with questions.

_____Introduce Excel with discussion: What is a spreadsheet? Name some spreadsheet programs (hint: Excel, Google Spreadsheet, Open Office). Why is it important to be able to use them? Prod students for answers that include:

- *Communicate information and ideas effectively*
- *Present relationships between information and ideas clearly and efficiently (from Common Core)*
- *Develop a coherent understanding of a topic or issue (from Common Core)*

_____Discuss the following Common Core goals and how Excel is uniquely qualified to assist in attaining them:

- *Make sense of problems and persevere in solving them (with Excel charts and graphs)*
- *Reason abstractly and quantitatively (numbers is what Excel does best)*
- *Construct viable arguments and critique reasoning of others (quantifiable arguments are defensible and convincing)*
- *Model with mathematics (demonstrate a scenario in Excel)*
- *Use appropriate tools strategically (When is Excel exactly the right tool to sort data)*
- *Attend to precision (with Excel's mathematical properties)*
- *Look for and make use of structure (formulas, charts, graphs)*

Best Practices

- *Use Excel to turn data into information*
- *Use formatting to make spreadsheet as clear as possible to readers*
- *Hone spreadsheet to audience, i.e., does data work better with tables or graphs?*
- *Collect like spreadsheets into one workbook*

_____What tasks are best suited to spreadsheets instead of word processing? PowerPoint? What spreadsheet programs have students used?

_____Display assessment (we use Excel, but you can use Google Docs or Open Office Spreadsheets) on class SmartScreen or make it available for download to student stations in read-only format. Give students the rest of class to complete. Students work by themselves (or you may decide in groups).

_____Walk around to answer questions that aren't skills related.

_____Remind students to 'save early save often' during quiz—about every ten minutes

_____When students are done, submit assessment via email or dropbox. Save to network; save-as to flash drive (why save-as?).

_____Those who finish early can visit websites on class start page that are tied into inquiry.

_____Using rubric on next pages, determine what skills class requires assistance with.

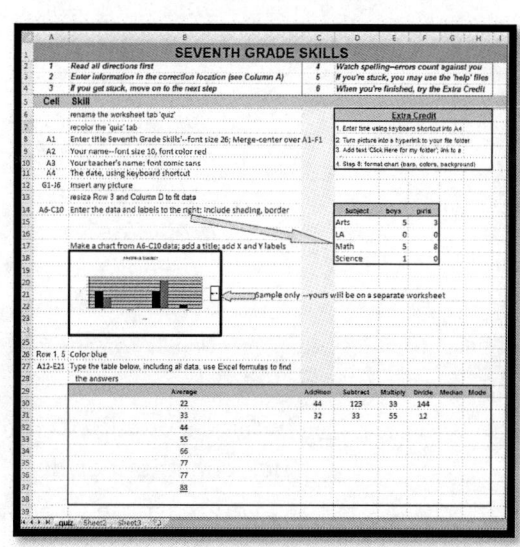

_____During second weekly class, review challenging skills. Review popular Excel shortkeys (at end of Unit).

_____Introduce 'formulas'. What are they? Students typically use add, average, alphabetize, but Excel offers many more. Point students toward the formula bar to explore. Discuss the most popular, i.e., standard deviation, Sin/Cos (Trigonometry), if-then arguments, PMT (to calculate the payment for a particular loan), depreciation of an asset, concatenations. Demonstrate a few.

_____Before wrapping up unit, discuss where students might find spreadsheets. In fact, they're all over the internet. How might this be useful? Demonstrate how these five locations (or others of your choice) can be downloaded and used:

- *NFL data (http://www.advancednflstats.com/2010/04/play-by-play-data.html)*
- *NASA Earth-Science (http://nasawavelength.org/resource-search?keywords=Clouds+and+cloud+cover&facetSort=1&educationalLevel=Middle+school&instructionalStrategies=Tutorial+program)*
- *Wind speed data (http://softwaretopic.informer.com/nasa-data-for-wind-speed-database/)*
- *Election Commission (http://www.fec.gov/finance/disclosure/ftp_download.shtml)*
- *Text data can be converted to visual data http://batchgeo.com/*

_____Reflect on what students have learned about spreadsheets. Prod them toward answers aligned with Common Core ideas:

- *Spreadsheets facilitate reasoning abstractly and quantitatively*
- *Spreadsheets facilitate construction of viable arguments*
- *Spreadsheets aid in making sense of problems and identifying a solution*
- *Spreadsheets allow for modeling problems*
- *Spreadsheets use repeated reasoning to solve problems, a useful strategy outside of spreadsheets*

Assessment Strategies

- *Assessment results*
- *Previewed material and came to class with questions*
- *Tried to solve tech problems before asking for help*
- *Joined class discussion*

_____Remind students to transfer knowledge to classroom or home.

_____Tuck chairs under desk, headphones over tower; leave station as it was.

_____As you teach, incorporate lesson vocabulary.

Extension:

- Play <u>Lemonade Stand</u> or <u>Coffee Shop</u> in small groups. Collect data in Excel and evaluate.
- Pick three-four formulas. Walk students through the creation of one (i.e., turning all cells of a certain value red). Have them figure out the rest by using Excel help files, Google search, other problem solving strategies.
- Discuss sorting data with Filter tool. Apply it to data students are using in class.
- Discuss Excel shortkeys at end of unit.
- Blog on Excel. If student don't have blogs, set up a Discussion Board with Excel-related question. This can be done as homework.
- Homework: Review Google Earth to prepare for next unit. Bring questions to class.
- Homework: Practice keyboarding with installed software, <u>Typing Web</u> or <u>Nimble Fingers</u> (Google names for websites).

More Information:

- For more ideas on tech assessment, read "14 Factors to Consider for Tech Report Cards" at end of unit
- Lesson questions? Go to <u>http://askatechteacher.com</u>

If you don't get through everything, check completed items so you know what to get back to when you have time later. I find as I focus on the central idea of a lesson, clarifying questions sometimes take more time than I'd expect. I'm fine with that.

Problem solving: If screen freezes:

- *Smash forehead on keyboard to continue...*
- *Enter any 11-digit prime number to continue...*

Excel Quiz

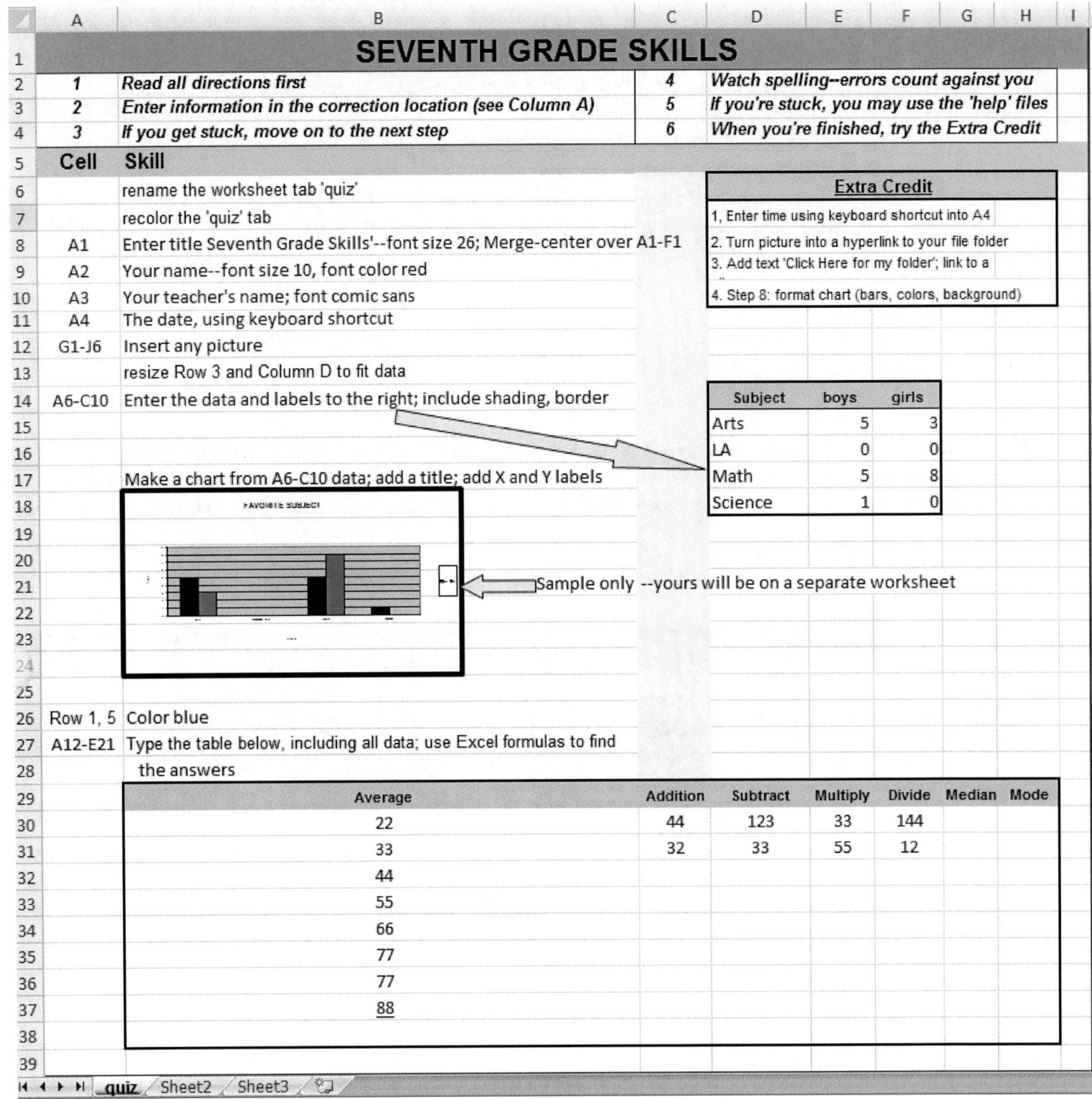

	A	B	C	D	E	F	G	H	I
1		**SEVENTH GRADE SKILLS**							
2	*1*	*Read all directions first*	*4*	*Watch spelling--errors count against you*					
3	*2*	*Enter information in the correction location (see Column A)*	*5*	*If you're stuck, you may use the 'help' files*					
4	*3*	*If you get stuck, move on to the next step*	*6*	*When you're finished, try the Extra Credit*					
5	**Cell**	**Skill**							
6		rename the worksheet tab 'quiz'							
7		recolor the 'quiz' tab							
8	A1	Enter title Seventh Grade Skills'--font size 26; Merge-center over A1-F1							
9	A2	Your name--font size 10, font color red							
10	A3	Your teacher's name; font comic sans							
11	A4	The date, using keyboard shortcut							
12	G1-J6	Insert any picture							
13		resize Row 3 and Column D to fit data							
14	A6-C10	Enter the data and labels to the right; include shading, border							
15									
16									
17		Make a chart from A6-C10 data; add a title; add X and Y labels							
18									
19									
20									
21									
22									
23									
24									
25									
26	Row 1, 5	Color blue							
27	A12-E21	Type the table below, including all data; use Excel formulas to find							
28		the answers							

Extra Credit

1, Enter time using keyboard shortcut into A4
2. Turn picture into a hyperlink to your file folder
3. Add text 'Click Here for my folder'; link to a ...
4. Step 8: format chart (bars, colors, background)

Subject	boys	girls
Arts	5	3
LA	0	0
Math	5	8
Science	1	0

Sample only --yours will be on a separate worksheet

Average	Addition	Subtract	Multiply	Divide	Median	Mode
22	44	123	33	144		
33	32	33	55	12		
44						
55						
66						
77						
77						
88						

quiz / Sheet2 / Sheet3

Grading Sheet for Excel Assessment

Excel ASSESSMENT

	Question	1	2	3	4	5	6	7	8	9	10	11	12	13	14	15	16	17	18	19	20
											STUDENT										
1	Spelling																				
2	Grammar																				
3	Rename tab																				
4	Recolor tab																				
5	Title																				
	Font 26																				
	Merge-center																				
6	Student name																				
	Font 10																				
	Color: red																				
7	Teacher																				
	Font: CS																				
6	Date (shortkey)																				
7	Image																				
	In G1-J6?																				
8	Table—data																				
	Shading?																				
	Border?																				
	All data?																				
9	Chart																				
	Title?																				
	X/Y labels?																				
10	Row 1—blue																				
11	Row 5—blue																				
12	Table																				
	Answers?																				
	Use formulas?																				
13	Cells right?																				
ec	Time in A4																				
	Image linked																				
	Link has text																				
	Chart format																				
	Total	0	0	0	0	0	0	0	0	0	0	0	0	0	0	0	0	0	0	0	0

Most Popular Excel Shortkeys

Alt + 0128 (keypad only)	*Enter the € (euro) symbol*
Alt + 0162 (keypad only)	*Enter the ¢ (cent) symbol*
Alt + 0163 (keypad only)	*Enter the £ (pound sterling) symbol*
Alt + 0165 (keypad only)	*Enter the ¥ (yen) symbol in a cell*
Ctrl + ;	*Insert current date*
Ctrl + A	*Select all cells in spreadsheet*
Ctrl + C	*Copy selection to Clipboard*
Ctrl + F	*Open the Find window*
Ctrl + K	*Insert a hyperlink*
Ctrl + Shift + :	*Insert current time*
Ctrl + Spacebar	*Select entire column*
Ctrl + V	*Paste selection from Clipboard*
Ctrl + X	*Cut selection*
Ctrl + Y	*Redo last action*
Ctrl + Z or **Alt + Backspace**	*Undo last action*
Shift + Enter	*Move to cell above*
Shift + Spacebar	*Select the entire row*
Shift + Tab	*Move one cell to left*

14 Factors to Consider for Tech Report Cards

It used to be simple to post grades. Add up test scores and see what the student earned. Very defensible. Everyone understood.

It's not that way anymore. Here are the factors I consider when I'm posting grades:

- Does s/he remember skills from prior lessons as they complete current lessons?
- Does s/he show evidence of learning by using tech class knowledge in classroom or home?
- Does s/he participate in class discussions?
- Does s/he complete daily goals (a project, visit a website, watch a tutorial, etc.)?
- Does s/he save to their network folder?

- Does s/he try to solve tech problems themselves before asking for teacher help?
- Does s/he use core classroom knowledge (i.e., writing conventions) in tech projects?
- Does s/he work well in groups?
- Does s/he use the internet safely?
- Does s/he [whichever Common Core Standard is being pursued by the use of technology. It may be 'able to identify shapes' in first grade or 'able to use technology to add audio' in fourth grade]?
- Does s/he display creativity and critical thinking in the achievement of goals?
- Has student progressed at keyboarding skills?
- Anecdotal observation of student learning (this is subjective and enables me to grade students based on effort)
- Grades on tests, quizzes, projects

I'm tempted to put everything in a spreadsheet, award a value, calculate a total and find an average. Then–Magic! I have a grade! It's risk-averse, explainable to parents and Admin, a comfort zone of checklists and right-and-wrong answers. But, I know I can't do that. In an inquiry-based classroom, too much is a subjective analysis, a personal evaluation of the student's uniqueness. I can't–and don't want to–get away from that approach.

What do you use that I haven't mentioned? I'm already thinking ahead to the next grading period.

Unit 7-8—Google Earth

Vocabulary	Problem solving	Big Idea
• *Dialogue box* • *Embedded link* • *Fly-to* • *Lats and longs* • *Layers* • *Overlay* • *Placemark* • *Screenshot* • *Tour* • *Voiceover*	• *My writing disappeared (Ctrl+Z)* • *Google Earth can't find what I'm flying to (is it misspelled?)* • *Tour doesn't play correctly (are locations in order?)* • *I don't have enough time for all the placemarks (reduce number)* • *I don't remember how I did something (check Help/Google Earth Communities)*	***Geography affects a country's history***
Time Required *180 minutes*	**NETS-S Standards** *3a, 4a*	**CCSS** *CCSS.ELA-Literacy.RH.6-8.7*

Essential Question
How can we use technology to understand history?

Overview

Materials

Google Earth, Problem Solving Board sign-ups and rubrics, keyboard software, Civil War websites (or similar), blogs/wikis/other online sharing option, project rubric

Teacher Preparation
- Confirm with classroom teacher that unit details align with their teaching
- Have Google Earth assessment rubric prepared
- Have Civil War websites on class internet start page
- Be familiar with Google Earth skills covered today
- Have project rubric available online
- Have Visual Organizer unit on class online calendar
- Have notes online for students to preview upcoming unit

Steps

_____**Required skill level for this unit: an understanding of Google Earth, including completion of at least one project.** If you've been following the SL curriculum for a few years, students are prepared.

_____Continue Problem Solving Board. Ask students if they have used solutions discussed in prior presentations. Any problems they'd like to share with class?

_____Any questions from keyboarding homework?

_____Practice keyboarding using installed software or online program like <u>Nimble Fingers</u> (Google name for website). Observe keyboard habits as students practice—posture, elbows at side, hand position, legs in front of body, all fingers used, no flying hands.

_____Any questions from homework? Expect students to have reviewed Google Earth unit and have questions. Use these as a springboard to lesson.

_____Students will explore Google Earth for the next two weeks and use it to study how geography affects history.

_____What is Google Earth? Have they used it in other classes? How might it extend learning? Here are ideas:

- *To model/explore issues (i.e., which geographic features impacted history?)*
- *To identify trends and forecast possibilities (Time Slider)*
- *To research (tours and layers on Google Earth, Google Sky, Google Mars, Google Moon)*
- *To develop cultural understanding and global awareness (photos attached to locations)*

Best Practices

- *Use Google Earth to visualize a location's geographic placement*
- *Move Google Earth locations from Temp file to a permanent file before closing*
- *Always back up 'My Places' prior to closing down*
- *Test tour before submitting*
- *Have 3D layer on for best view of locations*
- *Make lesson student-centered, student directed*

_____Discuss what students know about the Civil War—battles individuals, causes, repercussions. As students mention information, demonstrate how it is brought to life in Google Earth (find the location of battles, show geography of historic event).

_____For this Unit, students work in groups to create a tour of Civil War battlefields that 1) integrates charts, graphs, photographs, videos, maps with other information, and 2) highlights importance of geography to history (or choose a focus that works for your unique student group).

_____Provide at least three (or more, or less) locations that must be included, such as:

- *Location of Emancipation Proclamation*
- *Sherman's march*
- *Surrender at Appomattox*

_____Student groups come up with the rest.

_____Open Google Earth. Discuss and review what students know about program:

- *what is included on menu bar—file, edit, view, etc.*
- *what is included on top toolbar—placemark, polygon, ruler. Demonstrate how to switch to Sky, Moon, Mars. Show how to measure distances.*
- *what is included on sidebar—fly to, directions, layers, places.*
- *what are right-hand tools—compass rose, move, zoom, Street View guy.*
- *what is included on bottom toolbar—latitude/longitude, 'eye view'*
- *how do students drill down into 'My Places' to find file folders.*
- *how do students run tours.*

- how do students activate lats and longs.
- where can students find Help—Google Earth Help, Google Earth Communities.
- how can students save an image and share to G+ (if they have Google Apps)
- how can students add/edit/format a placemark.

_____Students have done most of these in prior lessons. You are reminding—not teaching.

_____On SmartScreen, play a Google Earth tour created by students last year (or one created as a sample). Notice 1) tour locations are in the same file folder, 2) tour goes in order of selections, and 3) tour can be activated, paused, and continued.

_____Remind students how to create a personal folder under 'My Places'. This is where they collect tour locations.

_____Demonstrate how to mark a location and customize placemark. Title is name of battle/event.

_____Dialogue box accompanying placemark includes 2-3 sentences that summarize:

- date of battle/event
- historic significance
- how geography impacted battle/event

_____Tour will open with a placemark where Civil War began. Dialogue box will:

- introduce team
- explain tour
- explain importance of Civil War (or similar event)

_____Spelling and grammar will be graded.

_____At least three placemarks include images as well as dialogue. Use 'add image' button in dialogue box.

_____At least three placemarks include resource links for readers interested in digging deeper.

_____At least three placemarks must include image overlays to represent historic figures.

_____Where significant (at least once), measure distance between locations (i.e., distance traveled between battles) and explain relevance in placemark dialogue.

_____Each class period, back-up folder to student network folder or digital portfolio (or email to themselves). This is critical because most school computers are used by multiple students.

Assessment Strategies

- _Anecdotal_
- _Joined class discussion_
- _Included required elements_
- _Transferred knowledge from prior projects_
- _Worked well in a group_
- _Previewed material and came to class with questions_
- _Backed up personal Places to personal folder_
- _Took advantage of GE's collaborative tools— Community, photos, more_
- _Took advantage of GE layers_
- _Completed project and rubric_

_____Once tour is completed, record it using GE's 'Record a Tour': Click on each location, wait for about three seconds, click on next location in sequence. You can also add a voice-over. Save recording to digital portfolio with a reflection.

_____Continually check for understanding. Expect students to solve problems and make decisions.

_____When done, run tour to be sure it works.

_____Student groups share their tour with classmates on SmartScreen, narrated to show understanding of events. They take two-three questions.

_____When students are done, discuss. What conclusions can students draw about the effect of geography on history?

_____As you teach, incorporate lesson vocabulary.

_____Remind students to transfer knowledge to classroom or home.

_____Tuck chairs under desk, headphones over tower; leave station as it was.

Extension:
- *Have students create a Google Earth tour that previews a field trip they are taking, i.e., to Washington DC. Include one fact about each location and a picture. Edit after field trip to include reflections.*
- *Other alternatives:*
  - *Wonders of the World tour (see insets on next page)*
  - *Immigrant's journey (see next pages)*

- *Math uses for Google Earth:*
  - *Distance between shore and continental shelf, or two islands*
  - *Height of building*
  - *Length of river (or a ship)*
  - *Volume of the Great Pyramids*
  - *Width of Grand Canyon*

- *Set up a wiki page where students can embed and share GE tours.*
- *Offer websites with Civil War data, images, background.*
- *Homework: Think about 'visual learning' in preparation for next unit. What are some examples? Bring questions to class.*
- *Homework: Practice keyboarding.*

More Information:
- *Love Google Earth? Here are more ideas for lesson plans:*

  - *Google Earth Lesson Plans I*
  - *Google Earth Lesson Plans II*
  - *Google Earth in Math*
  - *Planet in Action—Google Earth*
  - *Pompeii—via Google Earth*
  - *Google Earth—endangered animals*
  - *Google Earth—African Animals*

- *General resources on Google Earth*
- *Lesson questions? Go to http://askatechteacher.com*

If you don't get through everything, check completed items so you know what to get back to when you have time on later lessons. I find as I focus on the central idea of a lesson, clarifying questions sometimes take more time than I'd expect. I'm fine with that.

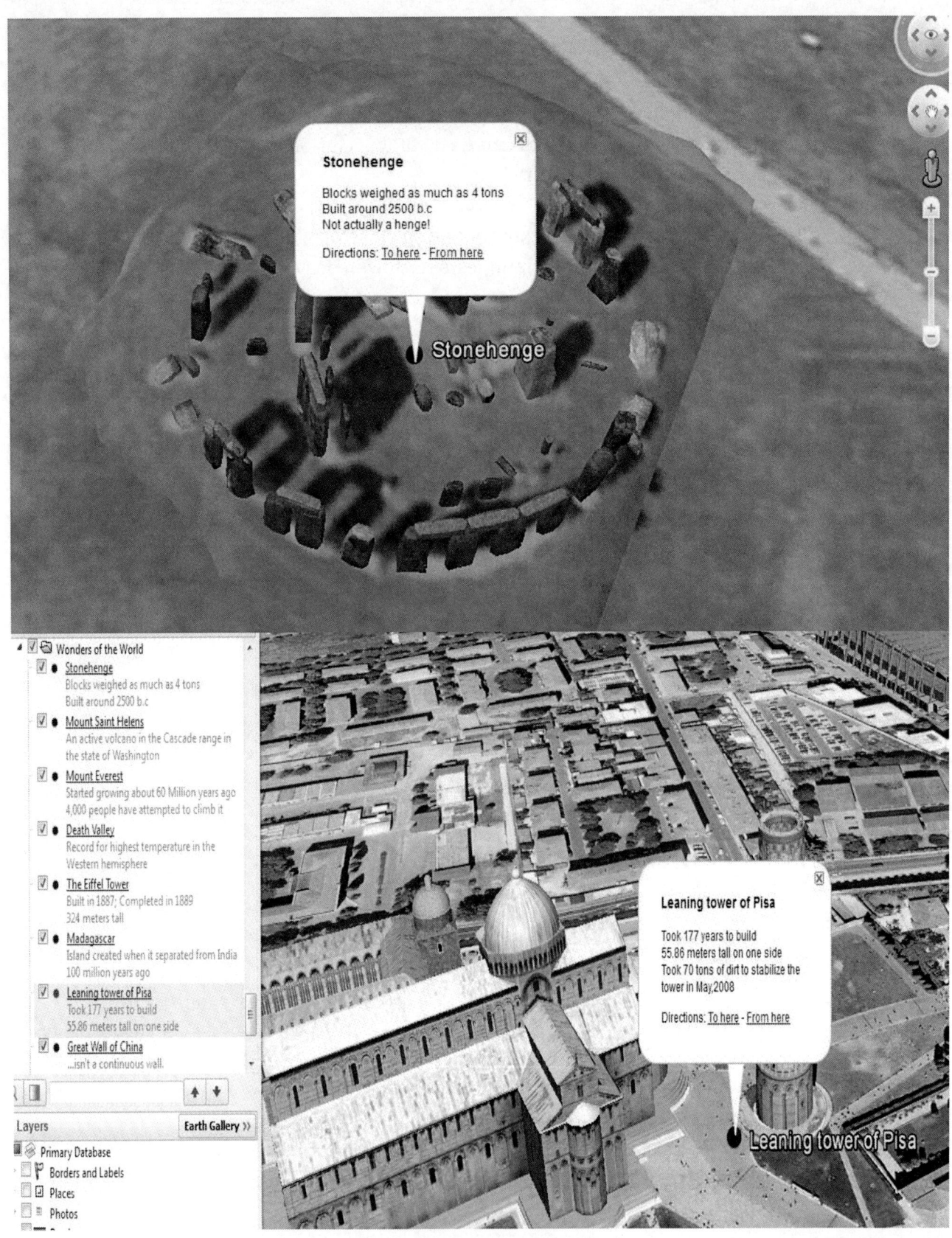

Civil War Google Earth Assessment

	Beginning 1	Developing 2	Accomplished 3	Exemplary 4	Score
Relevant Pieces included	Project includes some of required elements, but not all categories or all information	Project includes all categories, but not all required elements in each.	Project includes most of required elements. Those skipped seem to be because they were 'forgotten', not that creators lacked knowledge to complete	Project includes all required elements—4 battles, 3 events, dialogue box (with title and description), custom placemarks, 3 images, 3 links, 3 overlays, 1 distance, professional tour, embed	/4
Grammar and Spelling	There are numerous grammar and spelling errors, most of which could be caught with a simple edit process	There are substantive grammar and spelling errors, indicating that the creators did not do a final once-over before submitting	There are limited errors, most minor. Grammar errors are limited to those that indicate the creators may not know how to correct them	There are minimal grammar and spelling errors, none which could have been caught by an edit program.	/4
Knowledge of Events Evident	Creators made many errors in names and chronologic time, all of which should have been known to the writers by classroom discussion or research	Creators made errors in names and chronologic time, some of which should have been known to the writers by classroom discussion or research	Creators made few errors in names and chronologic time, most of which could be attributed to lack of in-depth research on the topic	There are no errors in events, people or chronology. The creators took the time required to get facts, figures, images exactly right, demonstrating a respect for themselves and the story being told.	/4
Technical Knowledge Evident	There is insufficient knowledge of the technology required to complete the required elements.	Creators seemed to struggle with the technology, but showed an effort to figure out how to deliver the required elements.	Creators showed an understanding of all required elements involved in creating this Google Earth tour, even those requiring self-teaching.	Creators demonstrated a deep and thorough understanding of all technology required to create a masterful and professional tour.	/4
Summative	Google Earth tour lightly touches on project theme (effect of geography on history), but does not effectively use the program's tech tools to emphasize important points	Google Earth tour points out importance of geography on history, but misses opportunities to use the program's tech tools to emphasize essential points	Google Earth tour sporadically explores effect of geography on history. Creators identify occasionally but effectively use Google Earth tools to emphasize salient points	Google Earth tour nicely explores the question (effect of geography on history). Creators identify relevant trends and use Google Earth tools to effectively emphasize salient points	/4

Google Earth Tour—England to the Colonies

Tour locations—include these spots and this information:

1. Your home in England
    a. Introduce yourself; tell us why you're leaving England
    b. Share your hopes and dreams
    c. Include distance from your home in England to the Colonies_____
2. Jamestown
    a. Tell me what would draw colonists to settle here
    b. Tell me about the jobs
    c. Tell me about the geography and climate
    d. Tell me about the organization of Jamestown
3. The Hudson Bay
    a. What is its impact on colonization and life in this area?
    b. Include width of Hudson Bay_____
4. The Appalachian Mountains
    a. What is its impact on colonization and life in this area?
5. Plymouth Rock
    a. What is its impact on colonization and life in this area?
6. Chesapeake River/Bay
    a. What is its impact on colonization and life in this area?
    b. Include length of Chesapeake River_____
7. The Potomac River
    a. What is its impact on colonization and life in this area?
    b. Include length of Potomac River_____
8. One colony from each region (northern, middle, southern)
    a. Tell me what would draw colonists to settle in each of these areas
    b. Tell me about the jobs
    c. Tell me about the geography and climate
    d. Tell me about the colonial organization of each area

Setup:

1. Set up a file folder in My Places, with your name
2. Customize placemark with your picture
3. Copy-paste each placemark for each location into your file folder
4. To edit a placemark, right click and go to *Properties*
5. Back up this folder to your network file folder

Immigrant Tour Sample

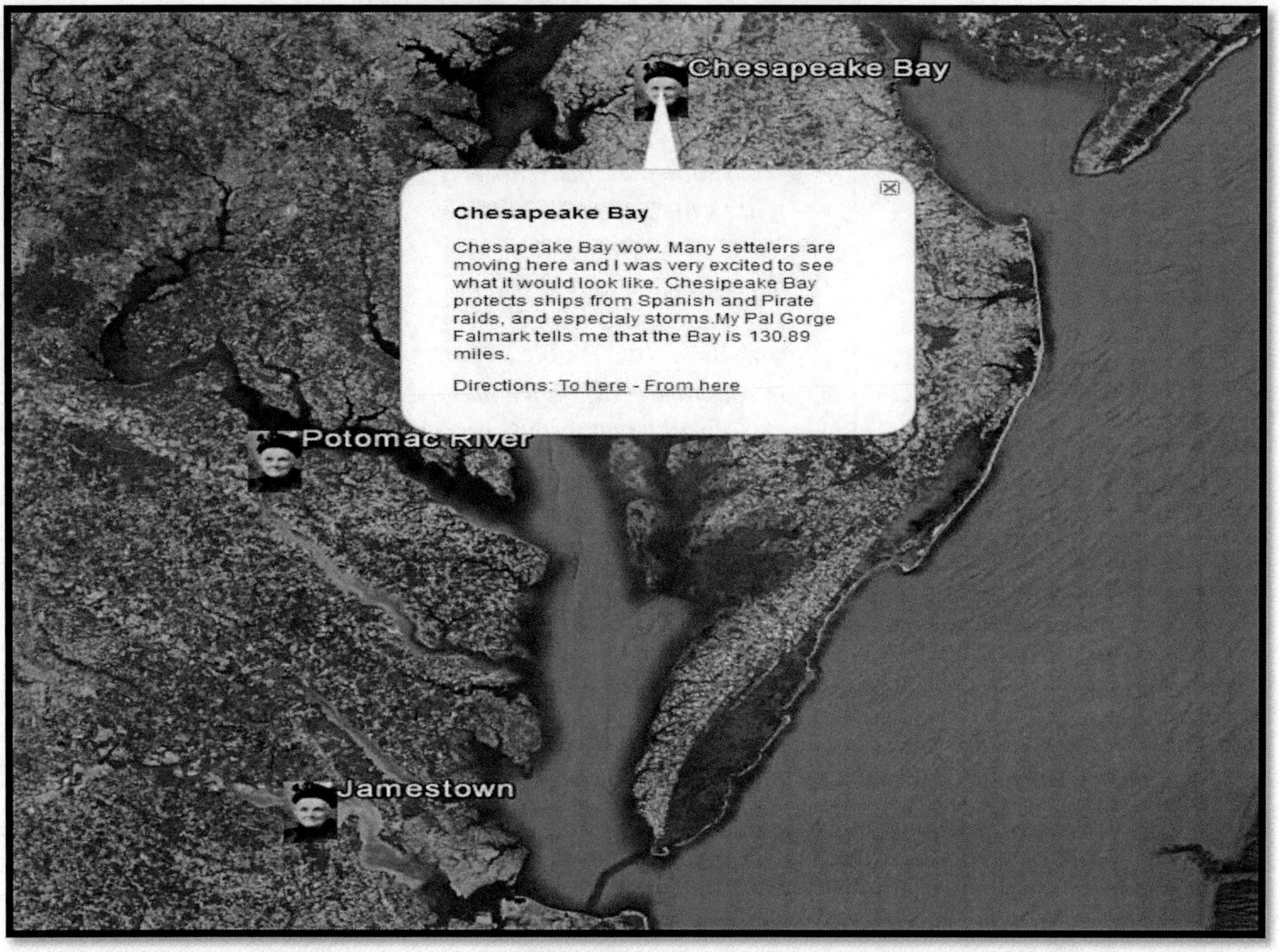

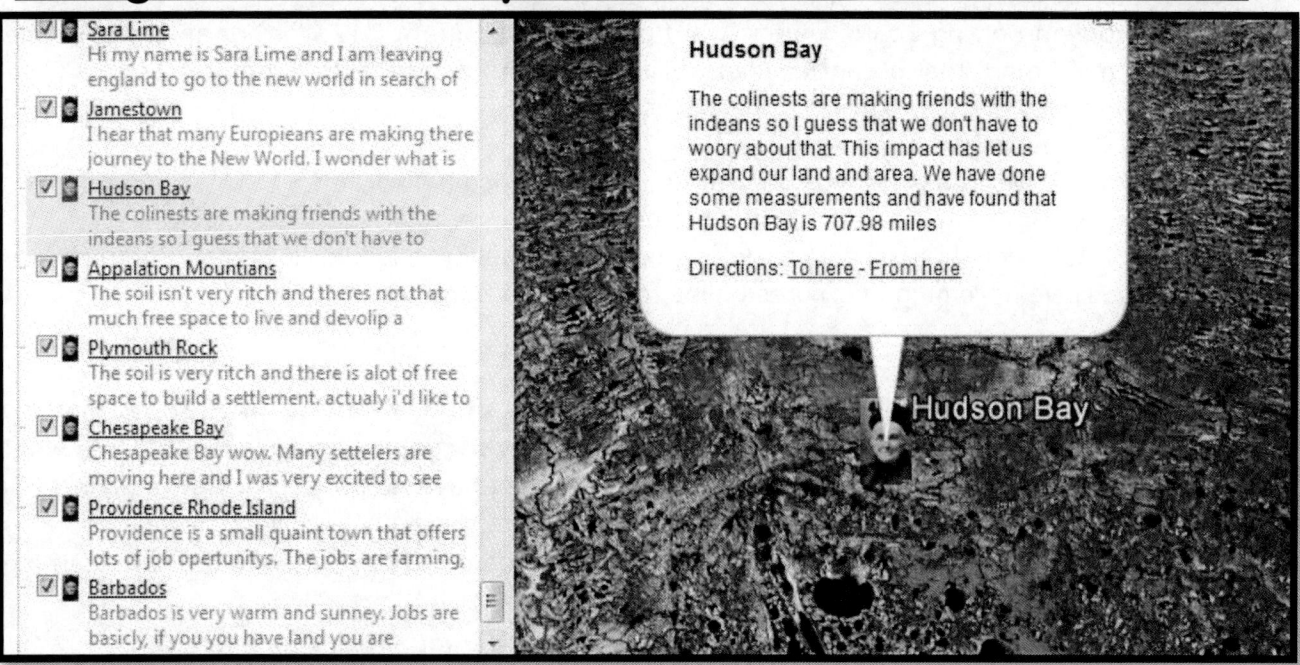

Chesapeake Bay
Chesapeake Bay
Chesapeake Bay wow. Many settelers are moving here and I was very excited to see what it would look like. Chesipeake Bay protects ships from Spanish and Pirate raids, and especialy storms.My Pal Gorge Falmark tells me that the Bay is 130.89 miles.
Directions: To here - From here
Potomac River
Jamestown

Immigrant Tour—sample list of GE locations with detail

Sara Lime
Hi my name is Sara Lime and I am leaving england to go to the new world in search of
Jamestown
I hear that many Europieans are making there journey to the New World. I wonder what is
Hudson Bay
The colinests are making friends with the indeans so I guess that we don't have to
Appalation Mountians
The soil isn't very ritch and theres not that much free space to live and devolip a
Plymouth Rock
The soil is very ritch and there is alot of free space to build a settlement. actualy i'd like to
Chesapeake Bay
Chesapeake Bay wow. Many settelers are moving here and I was very excited to see
Providence Rhode Island
Providence is a small quaint town that offers lots of job opertunitys. The jobs are farming,
Barbados
Barbados is very warm and sunney. Jobs are basicly, if you you have land you are
Hudson Bay
The colinests are making friends with the indeans so I guess that we don't have to woory about that. This impact has let us expand our land and area. We have done some measurements and have found that Hudson Bay is 707.98 miles
Directions: To here - From here
Hudson Bay

Unit 9—Visual Learning

Vocabulary	Problem solving	Big Idea
• *Background* • *Body language* • *Desktop* • *Diagram* • *Digital citizen* • *Digital native* • *Graphic organizer* • *Images* • *Landscape* • *Mind map* • *Portrait* • *Scholarly research* • *Tagxedo* • *Venn diagram* • *Visual learners* • *Visual organizer*	• *How do I open a program* • *What's the date (use shortkey)* • *What's the difference between 'save' and 'save-as'?* • *Why 'save early save often'?* • *I'm not a visual learner (empathize with those who are)* • *It's confusing (ask a friend to explain why they like it)* • *I couldn't get on keyboarding website (try other one)* • *Can't I write this instead (not this time. Imagine if you HAD to use images—no text)* • *What can I learn about a person from their body language?*	*Students use visual communications to share ideas in a clear, succinct fashion*
Time Required 90 minutes	**NETS-S Standards** *4c, 6d*	**CCSS** *CCSS.ELA-Literacy.W.7.4*

Essential Question

How do I use technology to communicate as a visual learner?

Overview

Materials

Problem Solving Board rubrics, word processing program (MS Word or an online widget like a mind map) that organizes ideas, visual program, mind mapping program

Teacher Preparation

- Talk with classroom teacher to tie inquiry to visual diagrams
- Ensure that all required links are on lab computers
- Add Digital Citizenship assignments to class online calendar in preparation for next unit
- Have upcoming unit notes online for students to preview

Steps

_____**Required skill level for this unit: basic understanding of graphic organizers; facility with online tools and/or word processing program.** Students who have used the SL curriculum for several years will have no problems. New students: Set up a time (after school maybe) to backfill where needed.

_____Any questions from homework? Expect students to have reviewed visual learning unit and come to class with questions.

_____Problem solving board—finish presentations (if not already completed).

_____Any questions on keyboarding homework?

_____Discuss concept of organizing ideas visually rather than textually. What does that mean? Hint: It's more than pictures. Remind students of examples completed in the past (Venn Diagrams, org charts, pyramids). What's the difference between sharing via 'text' and 'visually'? Can you blend both to make a more effective message?

_____First: What information needs to be organized? (maybe students are studying plot, characters, points of view from John Steinbeck's *Travel's With Charley: In Search of America*).

_____Second: What is the best way to organize it? A table? A graph? How about a visual organizer?

_____How might a visual organizer be uniquely placed to communicate (per Common Core Standards):

> ## Best Practices
>
> - *Remember Bloom's Taxonomy of learning styles? Many people are visual learners*
> - *Always present information to students at least two ways— one that is visual*
> - *Share visual organizers with neighbors; solicit their input*

- *Build strong content knowledge via visual media*
- *Respond to varying demands of audiences*
- *Use technology and digital media strategically and capably*
- *Help to understand other perspectives and cultures*

_____Here are several representative collections of graphic organizers:

- *Holt (http://my.hrw.com/nsmedia/intgos/html/igo.htm)*
- *Education Place (http://www.eduplace.com/graphicorganizer/)*
- *Education Oassis (http://www.educationoasis.com/curriculum/graphic_organizers.htm)*

_____Before continuing, discuss legalities of using internet images:

- *Review poster at end of Unit 10-12 for a summation of law. Discuss.*
- *Discuss second poster at end of Unit 13-15. What should students do if they want to use an image NOT covered by 'scholarly research' exception.*

_____Take as much time as necessary to answer student questions. This is an important and authentic topic.

_____Divide class into groups. Start with a mind map (see inset for example mapping a type of literature) using Bubbl.us, MindMaple, iMindMap, Spicy Nodes (Google for addresses), or other mind mapping program. Divide class into groups with assigned topic and brainstorm 1) what information are they trying to convey to readers, 2) how can it be presented as simply as possible, 3) how can it respond to the varying needs of audiences?

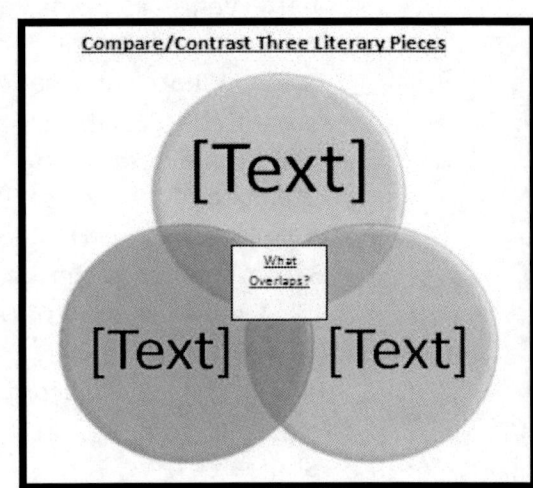

_____Next, completed mind map in hand, each group will produce three graphic organizers well-suited to share the information they mapped (selected from examples listed above). A hierarchy? A cluster web? Venn Diagram (see inset)? Other? Produce all three with coherent writing, making clear that organization and style are appropriate to task and audience.

_____Done? Share all three with a neighbor group. Do they understand your point? Which do they believe communicates most effectively?

_____Remind students to save early/save often.

_____Insert all three into a blog post and explain group's decision.

_____Comment on posts of three other groups and discuss why you agree/disagree with the visual organizer they selected, how it fulfills/fails to fulfill requirements. Remember agreed-upon rules of discussion (which also apply in a social media forum like blogging):

- *Express ideas clearly*
- *Build on ideas of others (both author and commenter)*
- *Make relevant observations*
- *Bring discussion back on topic if necessary*
- *Acknowledge new information expressed by others*

_____Remind students: Every time they use the computer, practice good keyboarding skills

_____Continually throughout class, check for understanding. Expect students to solve problems and make decisions.

_____Remind students to transfer knowledge to classroom or home.

_____Tuck chairs under desk, headphones over tower; leave station as it was.

_____As you teach, incorporate unit vocabulary.

Assessment Strategies

- *Previewed material and came to class with questions*
- *Joined class discussion*
- *Displayed creativity and critical thinking in mind maps and visual organizers*
- *Created and shared three visual organizers that fulfilled requirements*
- *Created a blog /article*
- *Commented on classmate posts*
- *Tried to solve tech problems before requesting assistance*
- *Followed agreed-upon rules of discussion*

Extension:

- *Discuss body language. Show how much you can tell about students by their hands, facial expressions, body movements. Provide concrete examples, such as:*

- o *What does it mean when a person is too quick to giggle?*
- o *What does it mean when someone looks up and to the left?*
- o *What does it mean when someone fidgets as they talk?*

- *Students who finish early can visit class internet start page for selected websites that support class inquiry.*
- *Homework: Review Digital Citizenship to prepare next unit. Bring questions to class.*
- *Homework: Practice keyboarding with installed software, DanceMat Typing, Typing Web or Nimble Fingers (Google for website).*

More Information:
- *Lesson questions? Go to http://askatechteacher.com*
- *Follow Digital Citizenship Curriculum (http://www.structuredlearning.net/book/k-8-digital-citizenship-curriculum/)*

If you don't get through everything, check completed items so you know what to get back to when you have time on later lessons. I find as I focus on the central idea of a lesson, clarifying questions sometimes take more time than I'd expect. I'm fine with that.

"Whether you think that you can, or that you can't, you are usually right."

- Henry Ford (1863-1947)

Examples of Visual Organizers

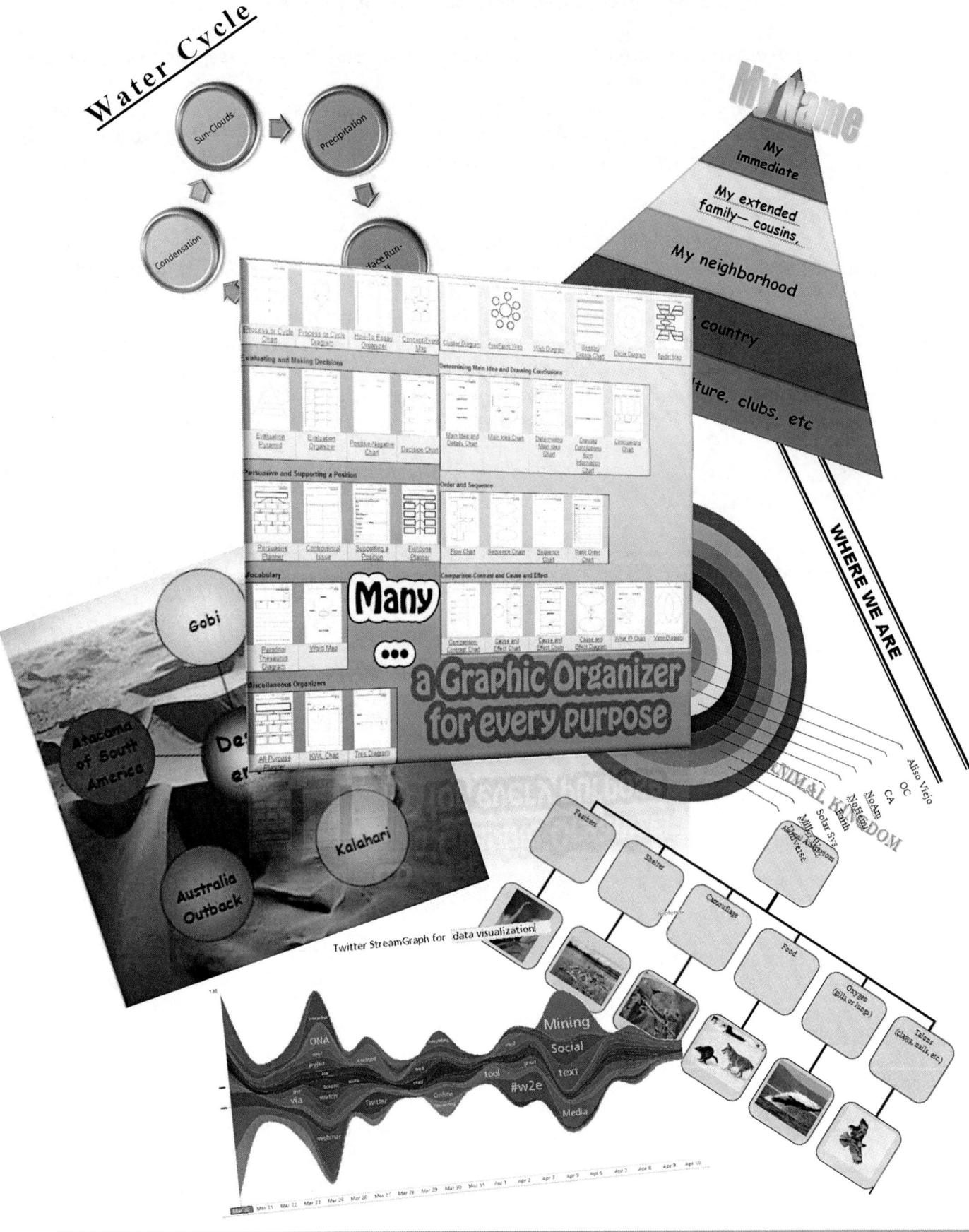

Unit 10-12—Digital Citizenship

Vocabulary	Problem solving	Big Idea
• *Benchmark* • *Click through* • *Cloud* • *Crack* • *Creative Commons* • *Cyberbullying* • *Digital citizen* • *Digital footprint* • *Digital native* • *Digital neighborhood* • *GPS* • *Hack* • *IP address* • *Keywords* • *Netiquette* • *Plagiarism* • *Social media* • *Spam* • *Touch typing* • *Wpm*	• *How do I share in Google Apps (click doc; share)* • *Keywords don't work (think deeper about topic)* • *Why do I have digital responsibilities when no one knows who I am (note to self: do the right thing even when no one's looking)* • *Everyone shares pictures (until they learn their lesson)* • *We were just having fun (does cyberbully victim agree?)* • *Parents won't allow child on social media (Pair up)* • *Why proper grammar in emails (it's not texting)* • *I can't find citation. Can I use text? (It depends)*	*Just as in the physical world, the digital world bestows rights and requires responsibilities*
Time Required *270 minutes*	**NETS-S Standards** *4b, 4c*	**CCSS** *CCSS.ELA-Literacy.WHST.6-8.8*

Essential Questions

What are rights and responsibilities of a Digital Citizen? What are implications of digital citizenship in today's world?

Overview

Materials

Internet, YouTube, student accounts for Glogster and BrainPop, optional account in Carnegie Cadets and/or Digital Passport, links to resources on class internet start page

Teacher Preparation

- Talk with classroom teacher so you tie into what they're doing in class
- Ensure that all required links are on lab computers
- Add upcoming graphics unit to class online calendar
- Have upcoming unit notes online for students to preview

Skills

_____**Required skill level for this unit: basic understanding of internet search/research skills.** If you've been following this curriculum for a few years, students are prepared.

_____Keyboarding speed/accuracy/skill assessment today. Warm up with installed software or online keyboarding. Review posture, hand position, placement of keyboard/mouse, best practices for keyboarding.

_____Open TypingTest.com or similar. Students select a three-minute quiz. Let them review webpage and determine how to do this (if they haven't done before).

_____Goals: 40 wpm by end of 7th grade. Type three pages at a single sitting (per CCSS.ELA-Literacy.W.6.6—from sixth grade). Review grading with students: It is based on improvement from first quiz—increased speed and accuracy, evidence of learning good keyboarding habits.

_____When finished, collect results for 1) wpm, 2) mistakes, and 3) competency.

_____A note on this **Digital Citizenship Unit:** it can be broken up and sprinkled throughout school year rather than taught as a unit. These topics easily scaffold 7th grade inquiry.

_____Goals for this unit include:

- *students understand human, cultural, societal issues related to technology and practice legal/ethical behavior*
- *students exhibit a positive attitude toward technology, a mindset that supports collaboration, learning and productivity*
- *students advocate and practice safe, legal, and responsible use of information (what's 'advocate' mean?)*
- *students understand 'digital footprint'*
- *students demonstrate personal responsibility for lifelong learning*
- *students understand part they play in preventing cyberbullying*
- *students use internet legally to gather information*
- *students use technology and digital media strategically and capably*

Best Practices

- *Remember both digital rights and responsibilities*
- *Use good grammar/spelling, not a texting hybrid*
- *Never share private info. Never.*
- *Respect all opinions, including your own*
- *Share what you know with the Universe*

_____Any questions from homework evaluation of digital citizenship? Expect students to have reviewed unit and have questions. This is a topic that intrigues many students, surprises others. Take as much time as needed on clarifying questions. The entire class session is fine. You will likely end up touching on most lesson plan issues—and more authentically.

_____When questions are done, watch and discuss Digital Life 101. (http://www.youtube.com/watch?v=e2QpzIAPXXA&feature=youtu.be).

_____Review Unit goals in light of this video.

_____**What are 'digital rights and responsibilities'**? Most students can come up with the 'rights'—access to the internet, use of information, creation of documents to be published and shared, freedom of expression—but what are 'responsibilities' of a digital citizen? Help students come up with:

- *Act the same online as in the neighborhood.*
- *Don't share personal information. Don't ask others for theirs.*
- *Be aware of your cyberspace surroundings. Act accordingly.*
- *Always show your best side online.*
- *Just as in your community, be kind to others.*
- *Anonymity doesn't protect you. You are easily found with an IP address.*
- *Share knowledge.*
- *If someone is 'flaming' another, help stop it within your abilities.*

_____How are online rights balanced by responsibilities?

_____Do you have to be honest if no one knows you aren't? If you're anonymous on the internet, who does it hurt? Solicit student ideas and experiences. Help them understand it's about innate morals—who they are.

_____Circle back on these concepts throughout year when appropriate.

_____**Next: online privacy**. Watch and discuss Tracking Theresa. How easy is it to find Theresa through crumbs left as she traveled the internet, thinking she was safe. (http://www.netsmartz.org/RealLifeStories/TrackingTeresa)

_____Watch and discuss the online life of a photo posted by an unknowing student. (http://www.netsmartz.org/RealLifeStories/YourPhotoFate)

_____Watch what happens to Eduardo when he posts what he considers innocent pictures— Two Kinds of Stupid from the national center for missing and exploited children. (http://www.netsmartz.org/RealLifeStories/TwoKindsOfStupid)

_____Watch and discuss Broken Friendship about two girls who share passwords. (http://www.netsmartz.org/RealLifeStories/BrokenFriendship).

_____Discuss the use of avatars to protect student privacy (see inset).

_____Wrap up with a discussion on hacking. Kids 'hack' game codes. Talk about this. Should they do it? Is it a victimless crime? What other issues should they consider?

_____What is the difference between 'hacking' and 'cracking'?

_____Expand digital privacy discussion into a conversation about Online Reputations. Watch and discuss Online Reputations (http://www.carnegiecyberacademy.com/funStuff/onlineReputation/onlineRep.html).

_____**Next: cyber-bullying.** Expand on last year's discussion with this website and this one (http://mediasmarts.ca/cyberbullying— http://www.childline.org.uk/Explore/Bullying/Pages/CyberBullying.aspx). Review statistics in Think Time: How Does Cyberbullying Affect You (http://www.youtube.com/watch?v=0oGFh0mwrjM&lr=1).

_____Watch and discuss <u>You Can't Take it Back.</u> What precautions can students take to insure they are kind and supportive online? (http://www.netsmartz.org/RealLifeStories/CantTakeItBack).

_____If students have blogs, with this discussion fresh in their minds, have them comment on classmate blogs. Good comments include a compliment, suggestion, question. Criticism is constructive and balanced. Conversation is on topic and relevant.

_____**Next: Digital Footprint.** Last year, students Googled their names to discover their digital footprint. Do this again. Has it changed?

_____Have students play <u>"A Tale of Two Footprints"</u> <u>(Google for address) and blog</u> about their online presence or lack of one. Which type of 'footprint" are they leaving? Comment on each other's posts.

_____Circle back on these concepts throughout year when appropriate.

_____**Next: Electronic communication.** This includes:

- *Email*
- *IMs*
- *Texting*
- *Cell phones*
- *Chat rooms*
- *Anything digital/online/without paper and pencil*

_____Review email etiquette:

- *Use proper formatting, spelling, grammar*
- *CC anyone you mention*
- *Make 'Subject line' topic of email*
- *Answer swiftly*
- *Re-read before sending*
- *Don't use all caps—THIS IS SHOUTING*
- *Don't attach unnecessary files*
- *Don't overuse high priority*
- *Don't email confidential information*
- *Don't email offensive remarks*
- *Don't forward chain letters or spam*
- *Don't open attachments from strangers*

_____Clarify terms like 'high priority', 'chain letters', and 'CC'.

_____Why is correct grammar/spelling important in email and not so much with texting? Hint: Consider <u>CCSS.ELA-Literacy.W.7.4</u>: *Produce clear and coherent writing in which development, organization, and style are appropriate to **task and audience**.*

_____Email is often required for online tools. Do students have one? Do they use parents?

_____Discuss 'spam'. What is it? Why is it sent? Cover these reasons:

- *It's a free way to find people interested in a product*
- *Sender earns money on 'click-through' (what's a 'click through'?)*
- *It gathers personal information*
- *It wears the receiver down until they finally order the product*
- *It spreads viruses that hurt computers (why do that?)*

_____What should students do when spam shows up in their email?

_____When students get an email, follow this simple checklist:

- *Do you know sender?*
- *Is it legitimate? For example, does the 'voice' sound like the sender?*
- *Is sender asking for personal information? Legitimate sources never do.*
- *Is there an attachment? If so, don't open it.*

_____Have students send a well-built email to a classmate (if students have email accounts) and reply to one they receive appropriately.

_____Is it rude to text around other people? <u>Watch and discuss this video</u> (<u>http://www.schooltube.com/video/31ce0fcb83a64139af1f/</u>).

_____Does school allow cell phones? What are reasons teens should have one:

- *Stay in touch with parents*
- *For emergencies*
- *So parents know where they are (via GPS)*
- *To collaborate and share*

_____What are reasons they shouldn't?

_____How many students' parents try to control cell phone use by:

- *Limiting their time on it*
- *Limiting the plan*
- *Having them share in cost*
- *Set up text-free zones, like dinner*
- *???*

_____Does this work? What would students suggest instead?

_____Discuss student responsibilities with cell phones, including:

- *Don't abuse them*
- *Don't overuse them*
- *Don't let them interfere with classwork*
- *Don't over-text*
- *Don't use them for academic dishonesty*
- *Don't use them for cyberbullying*
- *Don't use them to share inappropriate information*

_____Watch and discuss http://www.schooltube.com/video/31ce0fcb83a64139af1f/. Kids who walk with heads down as they text, talk, play games aren't paying attention to their surroundings. This dangerous habit lingers as kids get older and begin to drive.

_____What about chat rooms? Here are rules for chatting online:

- *parents approve*
- *student shares nothing private*
- *student agrees to leave site and tell an adult if it becomes uncomfortable*
- *student never meets an online 'friend'*
- *student screen name includes nothing linkable to student*

_____Circle back on these concepts throughout year when appropriate.

_____**Next: Digital Search**. Start with **plagiarism**. What is it? What can/can't be 'borrowed' from online sites? What are repercussions of 'plagiarism'?

> The law states that works of art created in the U.S. after January 1, 1978, are automatically protected by copyright once they are fixed in a tangible medium (like the internet) BUT a single copy may be used for scholarly research (even if that's a 2nd grade life cycle report) or in teaching or preparation to teach a class.

_____Discuss copyright law (see poster at end of unit and inset). Use a recent research project and share where students innocently broke law. What are consequences of infringing copyrights?

_____Some people want to share their work and collaborate with others to create bigger and better things. Watch and discuss Wanna Work Together about benefits of Creative Commons licensing.

_____Why pay attention to copyrights? How can students use Creative Commons in school and online (http://creativecommons.org/videos/wanna-work-together)?

_____Watch and discuss A Fair(y) Use Tale about digital security, copyrights, and fair use. (http://www.youtube.com/watch?v=CJn_jC4FNDo&feature=youtu.be)

_____Review **internet search/research** rules:

- *Add/subtract keywords*
- *Know about topic*
- *Evaluate websites*
- *Look for reliable extensions*

_____Watch this video (http://youtu.be/BNHR6IQJGZs) on internet search and discuss.

_____Google has created a series of 50-minute classes called Power Search (http://www.powersearchingwithgoogle.com/) including:

- *How to search*
- *How to interpret results*
- *How to find facts faster*
- *How to check facts*
- *How to put it all together*

_____Have students independently work through them (or cover in class if there's time).

_____Circle back on these concepts during the year when appropriate.

_____**Next: Digital Commerce**. What is 'digital commerce' (the buying and selling of goods online)? How can it be done safely and intelligently?

_____How many students have bought something online? If so, did they:

- *Check with parents first?*
- *Verify website was legitimate?*
- *Verify website was secure*
- *Feel safe because friends were shopping there*

_____Demonstrate what to look for by using a legitimate site like Amazon.com.

_____Go through process with students of buying something online:

- *They must have the money (even with a credit card)*
- *They must provide sensitive information (i.e., credit card number)*
- *Website keeps information and might sell it*

_____What are the pros and cons of digital commerce? Include:

- *It's easy.*
- *It's private.*
- *Products from other countries are available, even those in conflict with host nation laws and morals, i.e., pornography, illegal music, other illegal downloads.*
- *Website keeps your private information—or worse, sells it.*
- *Website could be hacked and your financial and personal information stolen.*
- *Website could take your money and provide no product.*
- *Website could steal not only your credit card but your identity. Discuss what that means with students.*

Assessment Strategies

- *Anecdotal observation*
- *Completed Google Power Search (if doing this)*
- *Completed blog posts*
- *Completed dig cit projects*
- *Joined class conversations*
- *Progressed in keyboarding skills*

_____Consider this scenario: 'Josie' sees a Wii online for $20. She knows that is too cheap. What should she do?

_____What is the best way to be good digital citizens and effective consumers?

_____Circle back on these concepts throughout year when appropriate.

_____**Next: Social Media.** What is 'social media'? Make sure discussion includes:

- *Facebook and Twitter*
- *netiquette*
- *parents*
- *student social media use*

- *student opinions of social media anonymity*

_____If you are planning to follow Google's <u>Curriculum: Understanding YouTube & Digital Citizenship,</u> start now.

_____What should be included on a social media profile?

_____What is responsible social media use? Think about digital rights and responsibilities.

_____What are long-term consequences of using/abusing social media? Think back to conversations about cyberbullying,

_____Watch <u>Teens Talk Back</u> (Google for address). Discuss as a class.

_____Circle back on these concepts throughout the year when appropriate.

Extension:

- *Create a Glogster poster on what it means to be a good digital citizen with links to resources. Include an avatar, a YouTube video, a Tagxedo of digital citizenship words.*
- *Blog about a video watched during unit. Why is it important to be good digital citizens?*
- *Create a map showing where student goes digitally on a daily/weekly basis. Connect locations with 'footprints'. At the end of the path, add a Tagxedo (shaped like a footprint—see inset earlier in this Unit) with all words and locations in map.*
- *Create PollDaddy poll on one of the topics above and embed into student blog or wiki. For example, for poll on cell phone use, student might ask classmates to select all that apply:*

  - *I can use my cell any time I want.*
  - *I often use my cell at meals.*
  - *I often use my cell in the car.*
  - *I have a limit on how much time I can spend on phone.*
  - *Other.*

- *Track where students found sources for class research project by placemarking on a world map. This will show how diverse we are in collecting information. Post.*
- *Draw a picture of a digital customer. Make pieces interactive, linked back to products they use and where to find them. Give proper credit. Include Ipads, iPhones, clothing bought at an online store, etc.*
- *Debate social media pros and cons. Tape and upload to class website or blog.*
- *Have students follow Microsoft's Digital Citizenship and Creative Content Curriculum (<u>http://digitalcitizenshiped.com/curriculumOutline.pdf</u>).*
- *Have students follow Common Sense's <u>Digital Passport</u> with units on cyberbullying, internet search, digital world (<u>https://www.digitalpassport.org/</u>).*
- *Students who finish visit internet start page with digital citizenship websites (<u>see list—http://askatechteacher.wordpress.com/great-websites-for-kids/digital-citizenship/</u>).*
- *Homework: Draw a picture using the most advanced graphic program student is proficient with (Paint, Photoshop, Elements, KidPix, other) in preparation for upcoming unit on graphics. Review notes provided.*
- *Homework: Practice keyboarding skills on online program with a goal of typing 3-4 pages in a single sitting, at a speed of 40 wpm.*

More Information:

- *Questions on lesson? Go to http://askatechteacher.com for help*
- *Track Digital Citizenship topics completed on "Here's What We've Done" at end of Unit*
- *Review copyright law (restated for 7th grade understanding) at end of Unit*
- *Read "How to Thrive as a Digital Citizenship" article at end of Unit*
- *Read "Will Texting Destroy Writing Skills" article at end of Unit*

If you don't get through everything, check completed items so you know what to get back to when you have time on later lessons. I find as I focus on the central idea of a lesson, clarifying questions sometimes take more time than I'd expect. I'm fine with that.

> **"Do, or do not. There is no 'try'."**
>
> **- Yoda ('The Empire Strikes Back')**

—From the Structured Learning <u>*K-8 Digital Citizenship Curriculum*</u>

HERE'S WHAT
WE'VE DONE
Cyberbullying
Digital Citizenship
Digital Commerce
Digital Comm
Digital footprint
Digital law
Digital privacy
Facebook
Fair use, Public domain
Image copyright
Internet safety
Netiquette
Plagiarism
Passwords
Social media
Digital Rights and Responsibilities
Fair use, Public domain
Digital search and research

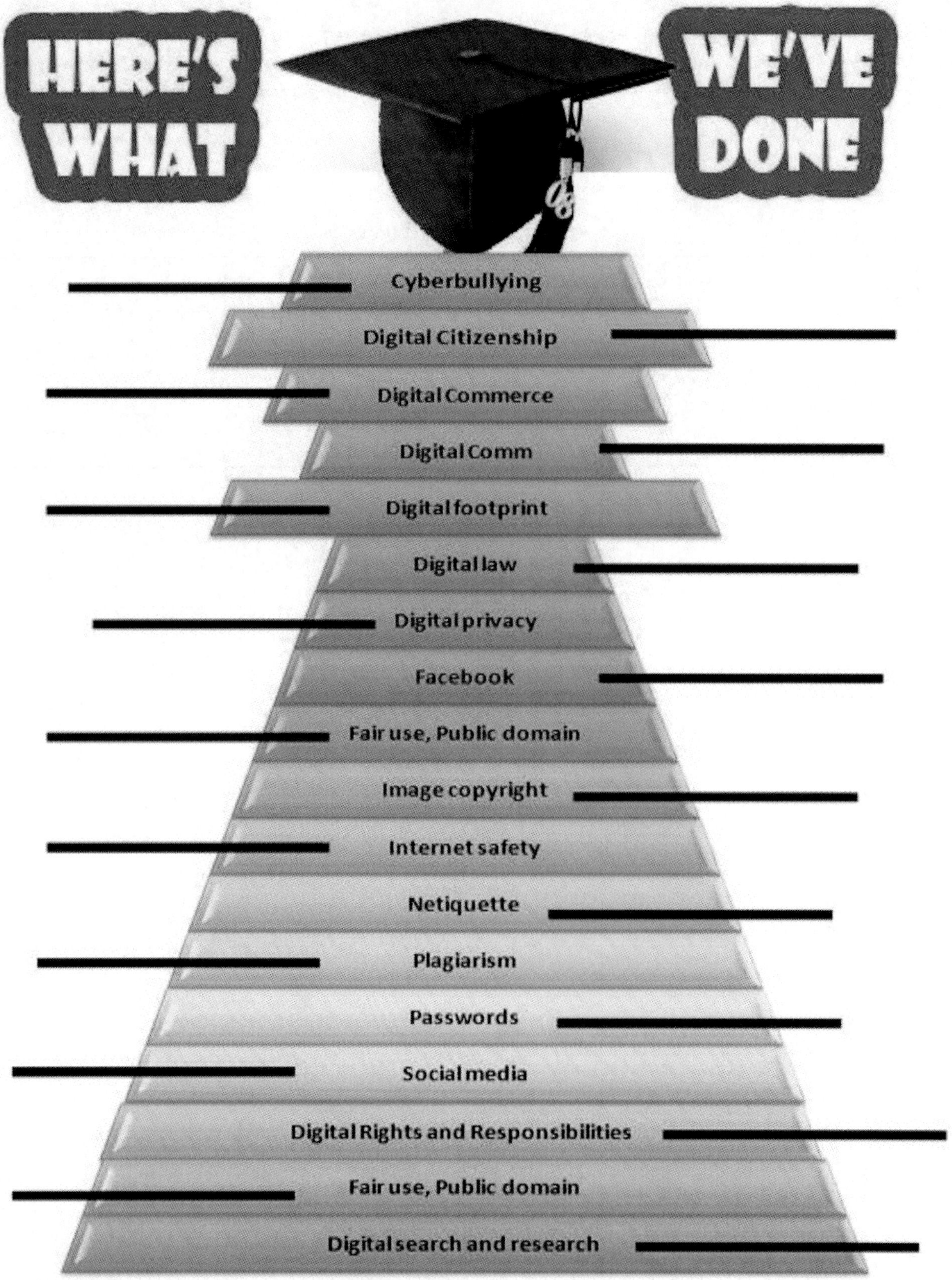

The law states that works of art created in the U.S. after January 1, 1978, are automatically protected by copyright once they are fixed in a tangible medium (like the internet) BUT a single copy may be used for scholarly research (even if that's a 2nd grade life cycle report) or in teaching or preparation to teach a class.

How to Thrive as a Digital Citizen

Thanks to the pervasiveness of easy-to-use technology and the accessibility of the internet, teachers are no longer lecturing from a dais as the purveyor of knowledge. Now, students are expected to take ownership of their education, participate actively in the learning process, and transfer knowledge learned in the classroom to their lives.

In days past, technology was used to find information (via the internet) and display it (often via PowerPoint). No longer. Now, if you ask a fifth grade student to write a report on space exploration, here's how s/he will proceed:

Understand 'Digital Citizenship'

Before the engines of research can start, every student must understand what it means to be a citizen of the world wide web. Why? Most inquiry includes a foray into the unknown vastness of the www. Students learn early (I start kindergartners with an age-appropriate introduction) how to thrive in that virtual world. It is a pleasant surprise that digital citizenship has much the same rules as their home town:

Don't talk to bad guys, look both ways before crossing the (virtual) street, don't go places you know nothing about, play fair, pick carefully who you trust, don't get distracted by bling, and sometimes stop everything and take a nap.

In internet-speak, students learn to follow good netiquette, not to plagiarize the work of others, avoid scams, stay on the website they choose, not to be a cyber-bully, and avoid the virtual 'bad guys'. Current best practices are not to hide students from any of these, but to teach them how to manage these experiences.

That's harder than it sounds. Children, as new digital citizens, feel anonymous in the vastness provided by the www. They think they can say/do anything and no one will know. But they don't yet know about something called a 'digital footprint' that tracks every step an individual takes across the internet landscape and—to many people's horror—forgets nothing. Comments made in high school, pictures posted in college, are available for a future employer to view.

Yes, this isn't learned in kindergarten. In fact, it takes me six years, a little bit at a time, before students accept these truths as their own.

Research smart

Today's students are expected to understand how to find information despite the billions (literally) of places to look. For example, if you Google 'space', you get over 4 billion hits. That much information is worthless. Students must learn how to whittle this list down to what their specific need is.

Collaborate with others

Where students used to have to find a common time that everyone was free, arrange to meet at someone's house or the library, and then share notes by copying them and passing out hard copies, now students can sit in their own bedrooms, or on their own laptop or iPad. They collect information, post it to a common document, and edit it collectively in one of many ways:

- via Google Apps—an Education account that allows for real-time editing of documents and enables teachers to see who's doing what
- through a Wiki—students collect all the information on a required subject in one spot and go from there
- for larger docs, a Cloud-based storage site like DropBox—invite group members to view
- with the teacher via email or the transparency offered by Google Docs (now, Google Drive)
- with subject experts via Skype
-

Share the wealth

Sharing used to be via PowerPoint slideshows, a written report, a student-driven play, maybe a poster. Technology has opened the floodgates of student creativity. Some Web 2.0 options for publishing are:

- blogs—post the article of all classmates and comment on each other's work. Then, edit the article to incorporate changes
- website—via Google Sites. If students have Google Apps for Education, this is included and requires no additional set-ups or log-ins.
- wikis—again, a great way to share information, videos, music, widgets of all kinds in a creative manner where presentation is as powerful as the content
- web-based tools (see below)

One of the most gratifying changes in my view as a teacher is the equity afforded by web-based tools. These online programs have flipped the classroom, turning student into teacher, making learning inquiry-driven, encouraging risk-taking rather than memorization. No longer does a family have to shell out hundreds of dollars for software because their children must have it for school. Now, there are a plethora of web-based, mostly FREE tools that record movies, sounds, turn pages into magazines, take polls, brainstorm, test knowledge. Here's a list of my classroom favorites, including:

- Puzzlemakers (prepare for quizzes)
- Voki (create avatars)
- Shelfari (share books)

It's not your mother's classroom—or even yours. With the advent of interactive textbooks and Siri-type voice input devices, who knows where we'll be in another decade.

Will Texting Destroy Writing Skills?

Across the education landscape, student text messaging is a bone of contention among teachers. It's not an issue in the lower grades because most K-5 schools successfully ban cell phones during school hours. Where it's a problem is grades 6-12, when teachers realize it's a losing battle to separate students from their phones for eight hours.

The overarching discussion among educators is texting's utility in providing authentic experiences to students, the type that transfer learning from the classroom to real life. Today, I'll focus on a piece of that: Does text messaging contribute to shortening student attention span or destroying their nascent writing ability

Let's start with attention span. TV, music, over-busy daily schedules, and frenetic family life are likely causes of a student's short attention span. To fault text messaging is like blaming the weather for sinking the Titanic. Texting has less to do with their inability to spit out a full sentence than their 1) need for quickness of communication, 2) love for secrecy, and 3) joy of knowing a language adults don't.

What about writing? In the thirty years I've been teaching everyone from kindergarteners to college, I can tell you with my hand on a Bible that children are flexible, masters at adjusting actions to circumstances (like the clothes they wear for varying events and the conversations they have with varying groups of people). There is no evidence to support that these elastic, malleable creatures are suddenly rigid in their writing style, unable to toggle between a casual texting shorthand with friends and a professional writing structure in class.

In general, I'm a fan of anything that gets students writing, and there are real benefits to giving students the gift of textual brevity rather than the stomach-churning fear of a five-paragraph structured essay. I've done quite a few articles on the benefits of Twitter's 140-character approach to writing and my teacher's gut says the same applies to text messaging. Truth, studies on this topic are inconclusive. Some suggest that because young students do not yet have a full grasp of basic writing skills, they have difficulty shifting between texting's abbreviated spelling-doesn't-matter language and Standard English. But a British study suggested students classify 'texting' as 'word play', separate from the serious writing done for class and results in no deterioration in writing skills. Yet another study found that perception of danger from texting is greater than the reality: 70% of the professionals at one college believed texting had harmful effects on student writing skills. However, when analyzed, the opposite was true: Texting was actually beneficial.

It's interesting to note that texting can be a boon to children who struggle with face-to-face situations. These 'special needs' students flourish in an environment where they can write rather than speak, think through an answer before communicating it, and provide pithy conversational gambits in lieu of extended intercourse. In the texting world, socially-challenged children are like every other child, hidden by the anonymity of a faceless piece of metal and circuits. Here's a heart-warming story by parents of an autistic child who found their first true communication with their fourteen-year-old boy via text messaging.

To blame texting for student academic failures is a cop-out by the parents and teachers entrusted with a child's education. Treated as an authentic scaffold to academic goals, teachers will quickly incorporate it into their best-practices pedagogy of essential tools for learning.

Unit 13-15—Graphics

Vocabulary	Problem solving	Big Idea
• *Artistic rights* • *Attribution* • *Copyright* • *Creative Commons* • *Credit* • *Derivative* • *Digital law* • *Digital security* • *Fair use* • *License* • *Mash up* • *Non-commercial* • *Plagiarism* • *Public domain*	• *There's a watermark on image (illegal to copy)* • *There's no copyright notice (doesn't mean it's free)* • *Can't tell if pic is copyrighted (then don't use it)* • *I can't copy picture (then find a different one)* • *I can't find my document/file (Start-search)* • *I don't have image software listed (try free online sites)* • *Video doesn't work (switch browsers)*	*The internet has a wealth of images that must be accessed carefully and judiciously*
Time Required *270 minutes*	**NETS-S Standards** *4b, 4c*	**CCSS** *CCSS.ELA-Literacy.WHST.6-8.6*

Essential Question

How can I use technology to produce and publish writing and present the relationships between information and ideas clearly and efficiently?

Overview

Materials

Internet, graphic editing program, blogs (or other online sharing tool)

Teacher Preparation

- Talk with classroom teachers about inquiry students can tie into images
- Do you have personal stories about the use of online images?
- Ensure that all required links are on lab computers
- Add Internet Search/Research unit to class online calendar
- Have notes online for students to preview upcoming unit

Steps

_____**Required skills: facility with internet images as well as drawing programs** like Paint, KidPix, Photoshop, Elements, or other. If students have used this curriculum for a few years, they will be fine. For other students, adapt expectations.

_____Have students had any tech problems they'd like to share with class?

_____Any questions from keyboarding homework?

_____Any questions on graphics homework? Expect students to have reviewed upcoming unit and have questions.

_____Throughout student education, they will use technology to connect ideas—often in 'mash ups'—and share with others. That can cause problems if not done correctly. Why? How? How do images play a part in communicating ideas clearly and efficiently?

_____What do students remember from last year's discussion on image copyrights? Some are licensed under Creative Commons (what is this?), but many have more restrictive licenses. What does that mean? What is the legal way to use an online image? Click inset below to visit Creative Commons license website.

_____What is the safest way to post images online? (Hint: Use your own).

_____If you have BrainPop membership, <u>watch</u> <u>http://www.brainpop.com/english/writing/copyright/preview.weml</u>. If not, watch 'Copyright Explained' (<u>http://www.youtube.com/watch?v=tk862BbjWx4</u>). Or both.

_____Review **'plagiarism'** from last unit. Discuss this video (<u>http://www.commoncraft.com/video/plagiarism</u>).

_____Discuss **digital law** as it relates to images, content, artist rights. Review:

- *Copyright law*
- *Fair use*
- *Creative Commons License*
- *Plagiarism*

_____Watch and discuss <u>A Fair(y) Use Tale</u> about **digital security, copyrights, and fair use.** (<u>http://www.youtube.com/watch?v=CJn_jC4FNDo&feature=youtu.be</u>).

_____Having grounded students in copyrights, plagiarism, and digital law, have them consider the drawing they completed for homework. How would they feel if someone stole it? What if thief posted it online? What if they made ugly comments about it? What if they made money off of it and didn't share it with creator. What if artist really needed that money to support a family or go to college? Discuss these ideas with students.

_____What is Fair Use? It provides rights to use images for purposes such as education without obtaining permission from creator. How does 'fair use' apply to student academic research?

> **Selected License**
> **Attribution-NonCommercial-NoDerivs 3.0 Unported**
>
> (?)
>
> (cc) (i) ($) (=)
>
> This is not a Free Culture License. ✳

_____Review legal summary from Unit 10-12.

_____Watch <u>Wanna Work Together</u> about Creative Commons licensing. Why is it important to pay attention to copyright? How might students use Creative Commons in school and posting online? (<u>http://creativecommons.org/videos/wanna-work-together</u>)

_____Anyone want to be an artist, writer, journalist, or other profession that relies on creativity? How might copyright law be important to you?

_____Show students how to use image websites like those listed below legally. Demonstrate how to access licenses and provide proper attribution (Google for addresses):

- *Pictures for Learning*
- *Creative Commons*
- *Flikr*

- *Free Photo*
- *Morgue File*
- *Open Clip Art*

- *Open Photo*
- *Pixabay*
- *Smithsonian Wild*
- *Stock Exchange*
- *Wiki Images*

_____I have found this is confusing for students. Many have never considered that they can't take whatever they want from the internet. They don't equate teacher admonitions about 'plagiarism' with images. *Aren't they free—they're on the internet* is common. Discuss until students are satisfied.

_____Creators of online media make decisions about what they will share with the world and what they won't. Respect that.

_____Discuss how artists share material online. What do these terms mean?

- *Attribution*
- *Non derivative works*
- *Share alike*
- *Non-commercial*

Best Practices

- *Always credit artistic endeavors (writing, drawing, photo-graphy, music, etc.)*
- *Ask permission to use material. Don't use if not given*
- *'Google' doesn't mean free*
- *Anonymous doesn't mean free*
- *Learn to use drawing programs to create your own artwork*

_____Discuss poster at end of lesson, "Want to use this image?"

_____One more concept: Hoaxes. Discuss how easy it is to fake a picture with programs like Photoshop.

_____Visit 'Is This Picture Real?' (or pick one that works for your student group). Why do students think it is or isn't real? Why might so many people fall for its message?

_____Watch video of War of the Worlds, one of America's most famous hoaxes. Why did people think story was real? Can you imagine coming in **after** announcer shared this was fiction? What would you think?

_____Conclusion: It's a lot easier to create your own graphics than use someone else's. Software to create pictures includes (Google for addresses):

- *GIMP*
- *KidPix*
- *Paint*
- *Photoshop*

_____Open school's graphic program. Have students draw a picture that collaborates with a class discussion (literature, history, other) and demonstrates knowledge of:

- *Formatting/editing in program*
- *Importing images to program*
- *Resizing/moving/cropping images*
- *Adding/formatting borders*
- *Blending image into a message*

_____When done, take a screen shot and share on blog/website.

_____Visit blogs of fellow students:

- *Build on ideas shared by their image with facts, descriptions, details that accentuate main ideas. Make connections.*
- *Demonstrate understanding of their perspective.*
- *Ask questions and/or respond to comments with relevant ideas.*
- *Follow rules of collegial discussions (see Common Core SL.7.1b).*

_____Have students use websites to create graphics online (Google for addresses):

- *Animations*
- *Art.com*
- *BigHuge Labs*
- *Dreezle.com*
- *Graffiti Creator*
- *Jackson Pollock*
- *Kerpoof*
- *Mondrimat*
- *Mutapic*

- *Odosketch*
- *Photoshop app*
- *Psychopaint*
- *Scribbler*
- *Sketchpad*
- *Splashup*
- *SumoPaint*
- *Tessellate!*

_____As you teach, incorporate lesson vocab into teaching.

_____Tuck chairs under desk, headphones over tower; leave station as it was.

Extension:
- *Do Webquest Hoax or Not and discuss.*
- *Draw a picture to support legal use of graphics. Post it to student blog or other method of sharing online (wikis, Discussion Boards).*
- *Have students find five images to support a project they are working on for another class (history, science, literacy, Language B):*

  - *One from a public domain website*
  - *One from Google images (that is legal to use)*
  - *One they create in MS Word*
  - *One they create in Paint, KidPix, other drawing program*
  - *One they create in Photoshop (if they have learned this program)*

- *Create a blog post that includes images from classmates. Provide proper credit.*
- *Students who finish early go to class internet start page for websites tied to inquiry.*
- *Homework: Review material for next unit, Internet Search/Research.*

- *Homework: Practice keyboarding.*

More Information:
- *Questions on lesson? Go to http://askatechteacher.com for help*
- *For more information on digital images, follow Digital Citizenship Curriculum (http://www.structuredlearning.net/book/k-8-digital-citizenship-curriculum/)*
- *Read "Where Can I Find Kid-safe Copyright-free Images" at end of Unit*

If you don't get through everything, check completed items so you know what to get back to when you have time on later lessons. I find as I focus on the central idea of a lesson, clarifying questions sometimes take more time than I'd expect. I'm fine with that.

"In theory, there is no difference between theory and practice. But, in practice, there is."

- Jan L.A. van de Snepscheut

<u>Want to use this image?</u>

- Credit Kali Delamagente@ Ask a Tech Teacher
- Link back to her website if you share it digitally
- If it's not for educational use—DON'T USE IT. BUY IT!!

Where Can I Find Kid-safe Copyright-free Images?

Dear Otto is an occasional column where I answer questions I get from readers about teaching tech. For privacy, I use only first names.

Here's a great question I got from a reader:

I am a computer lab teacher of grades 1-5. Do you have a good place for students to get appropriate and copyright-free images?

Let me address appropriate images first. I use Google as a default because it is the safest of all the majors (IMHO), not to say it's 100%. I spent quite a few hours one weekend checking out all of the kid-friendly child search engines (<u>Sweet Search</u>, <u>KidSafe</u>, <u>QuinturaKids</u>, <u>Kigose</u>, <u>KidsClick</u>, <u>Ask Kids</u>, <u>KidRex</u>, and more), but none did a good job filtering images. Content—yes, but images dried up to worthless for the needs of visual children.

So I went back to Google and tried their Safe Search settings. Normal Google search is set to moderate. For school age children, they can easily be set to Strict (<u>check out this video on how to do it</u>).

For some, even 'strict settings' isn't enough. Take the opportunity to teach students about internet safety, about what to do if they encounter something they shouldn't, about never straying from assigned websites. There's no way to protect children 100% from the world around them. Better we give them tools to survive and thrive, prepare them for the day we won't be there to protect their back.

Here's a list of copyright-free images. These are great, but limited in their content:

1. <u>*Creative Commons*</u>
2. <u>*Flikr—list restrictions— good learning tool*</u>
3. <u>*Free Photo*</u>
4. <u>*Google Life Project—from Life Mag*</u>
5. <u>*Morgue File—free, but check licenses*</u>
6. <u>*Open Clip Art*</u>
7. <u>*Open Photo*</u>
8. <u>*Pictures for Learning*</u>
9. <u>*Smithsonian Wild—200,000 of animals*</u>
10. <u>*Stock Exchange*</u>
11. <u>*Wiki Images*</u>

Unit 16-19—Search/Research

Vocabulary	Problem solving	Big Idea
• *Address bar* • *Alt+F4* • *Copyright* • *Credentials* • *Digital* • *Domain* • *Evernote* • *Evidence* • *Extension* • *Hits* • *Keywords* • *Limiters* • *Plagiarism* • *Quotes* • *Refine search* • *Search bar* • *Toggle*	• *My browser toolbar disappeared (push F11)* • *My browser window is too small (double click title bar)* • *My browser text is too small (Push Ctrl+ to zoom in)* • *I only want part of webpage (highlight, right-click, print)* • *How do I search internet (type into search or address bar)* • *How do I add keywords (use + or – to add/remove keywords)* • *I can't find copyright (try bottom of website)* • *It's difficult toggling between two sources to compare/contrast (Alt+F4 in two browser windows)*	*Internet research can be accomplished safely, legally, and effectively*
Time Required *360 minutes*	**NETS-S Standards** *3a, 3b*	**CCSS** *CCSS.ELA-Literacy.WHST.6-8.8*

Essential Question

How do I gather relevant information from multiple print and digital sources, use search terms effectively, assess credibility of each source, and quote others—while avoiding plagiarism?

Overview

Materials

Internet, website evaluation sheets, student Evernote accounts (if available)

Teacher Preparation

- Talk with class teachers so you tie research and websites into their conversations
- Ensure all required links are on lab computers
- Add Robotics unit to class online calendar

Steps

_____**Required skills: facility with internet searches and internet in general.** If students have been following this curriculum for a few years, they are prepared. For new students, adapt expectations.

_____Circle back to whether students have used solutions from Problem Solving Board. Any tech problems they'd like to share?

_____Take five minutes to test student keyboarding skills using TypingTest.com or similar. Remind students to use good habits, that goal is 40 wpm and able to type in excess of three pages in a single sitting.

_____Any questions from homework (review of digital search/research)? Expect students to have reviewed upcoming unit.

_____Discuss essential question: *How do I gather relevant information from multiple print and digital sources, use search terms effectively, assess credibility of each source, and quote others—while avoiding plagiarism?*

_____What do students know about this question from prior conversations, classroom inquiry, and personal experience? Break it into pieces and discuss.

_____Watch BrainPop Internet search video (search BrainPop site) together. Answer questions at end as a group.

_____What are three important search skills from video? Model an example using a topic being discussed in class. Say, students are reading "Blood, Toil, Tears and Sweat: Address to Parliament on May 13th, 1940" by Winston Churchill. Their assignment: Compare and contrast to other WWII documentation. What keywords would be useful?

_____Watch BrainPop Internet Sources together. Have students take quiz and email to you.

_____Again using Churchill's speech, determine its effect on wartime Britain; compare/contrast information based on **website extensions**.

_____Focusing on same topic, try search skills listed at end of unit, i.e., *what time is it in London, can students find a PowerPoint (.pptx) on WWII?*

_____Discuss:

Best Practices

- *Use keywords and limiters*
- *Use extensions to select reliable websites*
- *Evaluate author credentials before using as a source*
- *Know something about topic you are researching*
- *Spelling and word order matter*
- *Use Alt+F4 to search webpage for a specific topic*
- *Avoid sites with too many ads*

- *How can you use websites to answer a question if you don't know website is reliable?*
- *How can you explain an author's reasons and evidence, and/or identify which support which point(s), if you aren't convinced reasons and evidence are accurate?*
- *How can you integrate information from several texts (to write or speak knowledgeably about subject) if you don't know sites are knowledgeable?*

_____Watch and discuss this video (http://library.acadiau.ca/tutorials/webevaluation/).

_____Most libraries evaluate websites based on:

- *Purpose of site*
- *Trustworthiness of author*
- *Usefulness of information*
- *Up-to-dateness of information*
- *Ease of use*

_____There are a variety of checklists available that can be used:

- *Common Sense Media*
- *University of Wisconsin*
- *Cornell University*
- *Kathy Schrock's website evaluation*

_____Bring up a checklist on SmartScreen. Demo how it can aid in evaluating a website.

_____Have websites that tie into classroom discussion (say, on the underground railroad). Have students work in groups to evaluate based on prior discussions.

_____Next, students can work in groups to research a topic. Data will be collected from multiple sources, multiple media (video, oral, textual, images). Source selection will demonstrate that data is well-rounded, supports hypotheses with credible sources, that students understand topic, and enable students to fully answer question.

_____Students can use a variety of methods to collect information:

> ## Assessment Strategies
>
> - *Anecdotal observation*
> - *Completed research projects*
> - *Worked well in groups*
> - *Used a wide variety of sources*
> - *Understood importance of web-site selection and note-taking*
> - *Selected appropriate presenta-tion method for sharing research*

- *copy-paste to a notebook using Word, Google Docs, Open Office or similar. Leave it active on taskbar and toggle (Alt+Tab) between notes and internet during research.*
- *snip with Evernote (if school has student accounts), Snipping Tool or similar. Make sure students understand program function.*

_____Rephrase saved notes into words a seventh grader would use and credit source when student includes: 1) facts not commonly known or accepted, 2) exact words and/or unique phrase, 3) reprint of diagrams, illustrations, charts, pictures, or other visual materials, 4) opinions that support research, and/or 5) electronically-available media are copy-pasted, including images, audio, video.

_____Research done, discuss how students share/publish information. Should they use a word processor like Word, a desktop publishing program like Publisher, a presentation tool like PowerPoint, a video tool like Animoto, a poster like Glogster? Have students discuss options as a group, then select those best suited to goals. Share/publish in student blog, Site, class website, or wiki.

_____Throughout class, expect students to solve problems and make decisions.

_____Remind students to transfer knowledge to classroom or home.

_____Tuck chairs under desk, headphones over tower; leave station as it was.

_____As you teach, incorporate Unit vocabulary.

Extension:
- *Have students follow Google's 'Search Education' A to Z of online searches (http://www.google.com/insidesearch/searcheducation/).*
- *Have students play 'Search Shark' in Digital Passport (https://www.digitalpassport.org/).*

- *Have websites on internet start page that tie into inquiry.*
- *For more information on digital citizenship, follow K-8 <u>Digital Citizenship</u> Curriculum (<u>http://www.structuredlearning.net/book/k-8-digital-citizenship-curriculum/</u>).*
- *Homework: Practice keyboarding with installed software, <u>DanceMat Typing, Typing Web</u> or <u>Nimble Fingers</u> (Google for website).*
- *Homework: Review preparatory material on 'Robotics' for next unit.*

More Information:
- *Lesson questions? Go to <u>http://askatechteacher.com</u>*
- *Follow keyboard lessons in <u>K-8 Keyboard Curriculum</u> (<u>http://structuredlearning.net/k8keyboardcurriculum.html</u>)*

If you don't get through everything, check completed items so you know what to get back to when you have time on later lessons. I find as I focus on the central idea of a lesson, clarifying questions sometimes take more time than I'd expect. I'm fine with that.

"The difference between 'involvement' and 'commitment' is like an eggs-and-ham breakfast: the chicken was 'involved' - the pig was 'committed'."

- unknown

HOW TO SEARCH ON GOOGLE

Definitions	Define:computer definitions of the word **computer** from Web.
Phonebook	'phonebook:Murray Irvine' Phonebook for people named 'murray' in Irvine
Calculator	33 + 33 provides the answer to any function
File type finder	filetype:ppt "civil war" finds PowerPoints on Civil War
Site type finder	Site:edu Lincoln finds .edu websites about Lincoln
Similar sites	related:www.google.com (or the website you want related)
License plate finder	Type plate number into search bar
Time finder	'time in New York' tells you current time in New York

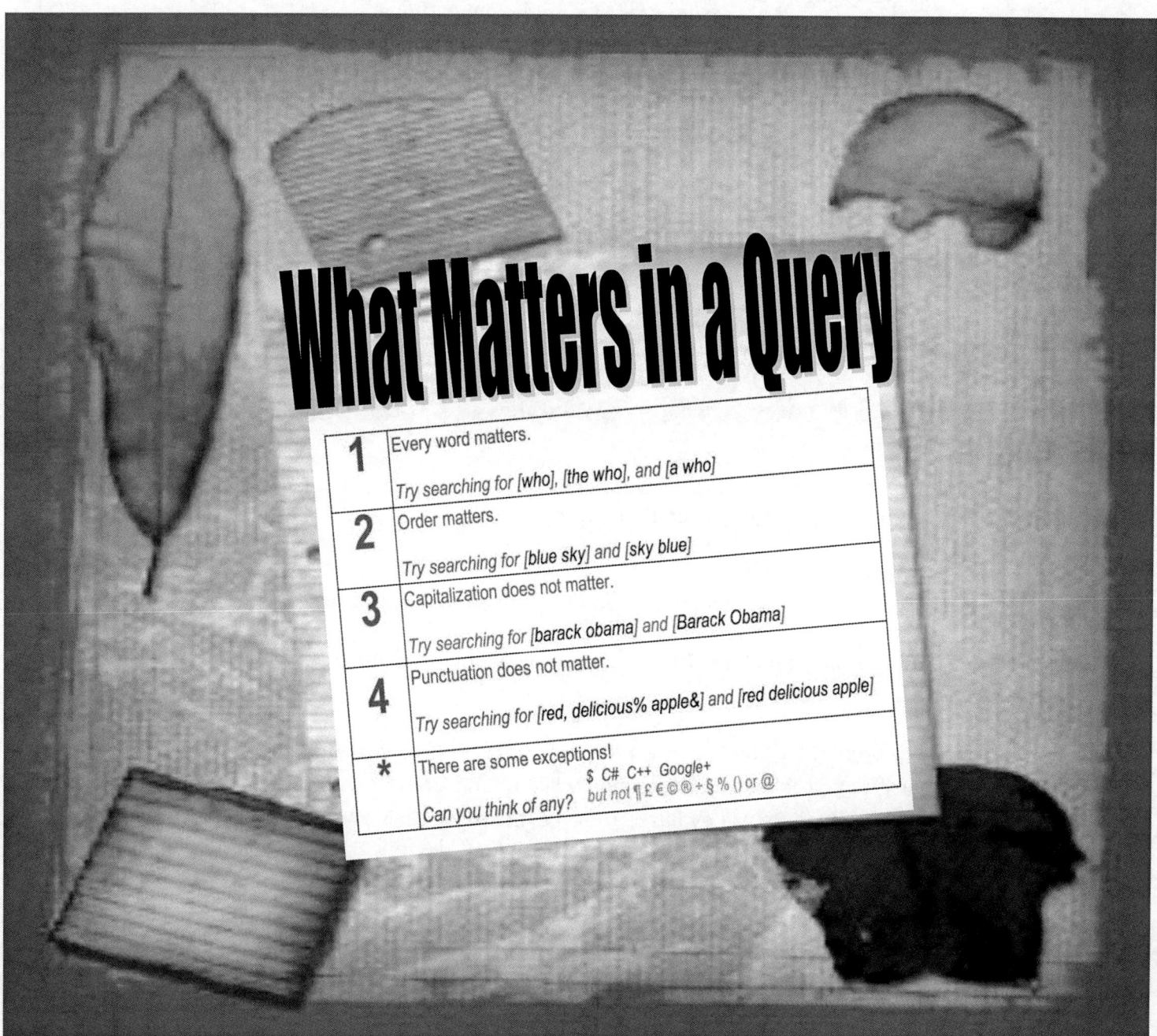

What Matters in a Query

1	Every word matters.
	Try searching for [who], [the who], and [a who]
2	Order matters.
	Try searching for [blue sky] and [sky blue]
3	Capitalization does not matter.
	Try searching for [barack obama] and [Barack Obama]
4	Punctuation does not matter.
	Try searching for [red, delicious% apple&] and [red delicious apple]
*	There are some exceptions!
	$ C# C++ Google+
	but not ¶ £ € © ® + § % () or @
	Can you think of any?

Week 20-23—Robotics

Vocabulary	Problem solving	Big Idea
• *Angle beams* • *Block* • *Bot* • *Debug* • *Forever loops* • *Fun* • *Loops* • *NXT* • *Rigid construction* • *Pegs* • *Pre-programming* • *Qualitative* • *Quantitative* • *Robotics* • *Screenshot* • *Sensor* • *Sentient* • *Ultrasonic sensor*	• *Website address won't link (push spacebar after address) Still won't work (does it start with 'http://'?)* • *What does 'Save early-save often' mean? (Ctrl+S often to save data)* • *I don't know how to *** (try different strategies)* • *My robotics program doesn't work. (debug. Go through all steps to find mistake)* • *I like building robots, but not other stuff (this unit's more about 'other stuff' than 'building')* • *My teammates aren't working as hard as I am* • *I have to run back-and-forth to computer and robot for instructions (use iPad)*	*Technology enables me to control devices that make life easier, better, more productive*
Time Required *360 minutes*	**NETS-S Standards** *3b, 4b*	**CCSS** *CCSS.Math.Practice.MP*

Essential Question

How can I use technology to create digital devices that make life better (and what is 'better'?)

Overview

Materials

Robotics equipment, NXT programming software (or similar), pieces required for simulations, keyboarding speed quiz website

Teacher Preparation

- Talk with classroom teacher so you tie into their science and math inquiry
- Ensure required links are on lab computers
- Add Pre-programming/Scratch unit to class online calendar

Steps

_____**No specific skills required in preparation of this unit.**

_____Any tech problems students would like to share?

_____Today, students will evaluate their keyboarding skills. Warm up with installed software or online keyboarding program. Review posture, hand position, placement of keyboard/mouse, best practices for keyboarding.

_____Don't look at keys; keep fingers on home row and elbows at sides. Grading based on improvement from last quiz. You want evidence of learning.

_____Goals: 1) 40 wpm by end of 7th grade with good sills, and 2) type three pages at a single sitting (per CCSS.ELA-Literacy.W.6.6).

_____Open TypingTest.com or similar. Students select a three-minute quiz.

_____When finished, review results for 1) wpm, 2) errors, and 3) competency. Collect results as students finish.

_____Any homework questions on robots and robotics? Expect students to have some.

_____Why learn 'robotics? If students have used robots (Lego Mindstorm et al), what have they learned from them? Take time on this question. Transfer is at the core of why we teach topics like robotics, games, and Scratch. Prod students to come up with:

- *Thinking skills*
- *Problem-solving skills*
- *Critical thinking*
- *Application of learned math*

_____Common Core Standards for Mathematical Practice list traits necessary to succeed in math. But these criteria are about more than math: They are fundamental to life's daily decisions—to evaluate new circumstances and determine a direction, to consider possible paths to an end and select the most likely to succeed, to mull over new ideas and fit them into accepted constructs. These are difficult to teach unless part of a larger process—like next three units—Robotics, Scratch, and Programming.

_____Discuss the meaning of:

Best Practices

- *Don't share robots. Each group has their own*
- *If a robot doesn't do what you thought it would, re-evaluate and try again*
- *Post and review class rules.*
- *Watch Group Dynamics and head off potential problems*
- *"Clean up as you work" is important. Model this during activities. Allow plenty of clean up time at end.*

- **Make sense of problems and persevere in solving them**—*robot does what it is told. Students must identify problem, find programming error, and fix it.*
- **Reason abstractly and quantitatively**—*robot program is based on symbols. This requires ability to visualize results as well as an abstract understanding of what is occurring.*
- **Construct viable arguments and critique reasoning of others**—*'Garbage in garbage out' remains the motto of programming. If a script fails to achieve desired results, work as a team to critique process. And, help neighbors if they are stuck.*
- **Model with mathematics**—*debugging scripts is not unlike decoding a mathematics formula.*
- **Use appropriate tools strategically**—*NXT program offers a plethora of scripts, blocks, tools. Adapt them strategically to unique needs.*
- **Attend to precision**—*again, 'garbage in garbage out'. For the program to accomplish what students want requires patience and precision.*
- **Look for and make use of structure**—*look at available tools, scripts, blocks, options, and select those that facilitate student needs*

- **Look for and express regularity in repeated reasoning**—*notice when a formula/program/script repeats itself (and use the Forever Loop). This provides shortcuts to goals.*

_____Specific goals of this unit include:

- *How do we create a robot?*
- *How do we program it to do what is needed?*
- *How do we problem-solve if/when it doesn't work correctly?*
- *How do we work collaboratively in accomplishing a common goal?*

_____Make theme authentic for students. A good example is this <u>NASA lesson plan on Mars</u>. Students create their version of Curiosity and explore the Red Planet.

_____Before beginning, discuss: What are robots? What are their uses? Write answers on SmartScreen as class brainstorms.

_____ Why are robots so appealing? Discuss popular robots like:

- *7 of 9 (Borg in Star Trek)*
- *Bomb Disposal robots*
- *C-3PO and R2-D2*
- *Daleks (from Dr. Who)*
- *Data (from StarTrek)*
- *Consumer robots*
- *I, Robot (Asimov)*
- *Industrial robots*
- *Lost in Space robot*
- *Mars Curiosity*
- *Marvin the Paranoid Android (Hitchhiker's Guide to the Galaxy)*
- *Mining robots*
- *Tin Man (Oz)*
- *Transformers*

_____Show a sample of robot students will build. What are main parts:

- *A movable physical structure*
- *A sensor system*
- *A power supply*
- *A computer "brain" to control parts*

_____Place students in groups. Pass out box of parts. Let students play without mixing them up.

_____Review parts.

_____Review NXT user guide. If students have iPads, load guide into iBooks or Kindle (or similar reading app). Review (intro, software, technology, parts list, building guide).

_____Demonstrate how to build a basic robot by reading directions and identifying required parts. This is what you'll expect them to do. Students with the engineering gene will love this part!

_____Discuss how robot knows what to do. How do humans know what to do? Animals? The TV at home? The computer? What's the difference between a 'sentient' being and one that is 'non-sentient'? Anyone see Matrix?

_____This robot isn't sentient, so will only do what it's told. Students do so via programming software.

_____Give students time to review NXT Programming software (Lego Mindstorm Education NXT Programming—see first inset), test, try things, see what happens. This is fun if they're more geek than engineer.

_____Create a sample program with student help (see second inset). Compare it to Algebraic expressions students work with in math.

_____Depending upon student group, they can either observe or work with you.

_____Demonstrate how to upload program to robot.

_____Students now build their robot and program it.

_____Each group must complete five tasks. Here's a sample list or ad those that work for your students:

- go in reverse
- accelerate
- turn
- detect sound
- detect touch

_____This is a student-directed unit, student-paced. You guide, provide an overview, but students are expected to use available resources to figure out tasks independent of teacher direction. Why? This will be expected in high school, college, future jobs. This is problem solving.

_____Besides core robot, students must learn to attach and use parts such as:

- Forklift arm
- Karate arm and chopping block
- Kicker and long arm
- Pusher

_____When a group thinks they have completed a task, teacher observes. The group has three tries to correctly complete task.

_____Don't be surprised if students come up with questions you don't know the answer to. The joy of tech is exploration—finding answers to new questions. Remind students this is fun, and they should not be surprised if they must:

- *Improvise*
- *Change the rules*
- *Try things they don't know the answer to*

In fact, you want this to happen.

_____Throughout robotics, expect students to blog about their efforts. What works? What problems do they encounter? Get help from school blogger community. Take pictures and videos of what they're doing and share. Comment on posts of others. Answer questions. Applaud successes. Follow class discussion rules.

_____Culmination of unit is <u>Bot Battles</u>. Create a ring with masking tape on carpet. Place two robots in ring (that are programmed to push opponent out of ring). Start their programs and see what happens.

_____What strategies are required to battle another bot? For example:

- *Success is highly dependent upon construction. Discuss what elements might make a robot more/less successful. When a bot loses, evaluate why.*
- *Using a light sensor to detect ring border is a typical starting point, but more sophisticated robots might use touch or ultrasonic sensor to detect a robot. Try these.*

_____Use Tournament Elimination poster at end of unit for tracking Challenges if desired. It's created in Excel (column/row designations are included).

_____If desired, award certificates (see sample at end of lesson) for participation and accomplishment.

_____Remind students to transfer knowledge to classroom or home.

_____Tuck chairs under desk, headphones over tower; leave station as it was.

_____As you teach, incorporate lesson vocabulary.

Assessment Strategies

- *Completed robot tasks*
- *Debugged program*
- *Participated in Bot Battles*
- *Learned problem solving*

Extension:

- *If both robots use ultrasonic sensor, they might interfere and confuse each other. Be aware of this.*
- *If student forgets where to find programs on robot, see diagram at end of lesson.*
- *Pick one of <u>14 options on NASA's Mars Education website</u> to engage students. A few favorites: 1) create a Mars community, and 2) Rover Races.*

- Enter a robotics competition as a school team.
- Ask students to analyze how robots know what to do? How do they know where they are? How do they know where to go? How do they control their 'bodies'? How might they see the world? (from Carnegie Mellon grad student David S. Touretzky's paper, "_Seven Big Ideas in Robotics, and How To Teach Them_")
- Find hints and tricks at _NxtPrograms.com._
- Homework: Practice keyboarding with installed software, _DanceMat Typing, Typing Web_ or _Nimble Fingers_ (Google for website).
- Homework: Review prep material on Scratch and pre-programming for next unit.

More Information:
- For introductory robotics training materials, visit Carnegie Mellon's _NXT Video Trainer_
- Lesson questions? Go to_http://askatechteacher.com_
- Follow keyboard lessons in _K-8 Keyboard Curriculum_ (_http://structuredlearning.net/k8keyboardcurriculum.html_)

If you don't get through everything, check completed items so you know what to get back to when you have time on later lessons. I find as I focus on the central idea of a lesson, clarifying questions sometimes take more time than I'd expect. I'm fine with that. There'll be lessons later that move faster than I planned.

Image Credit: Dave at NxtPrograms.com

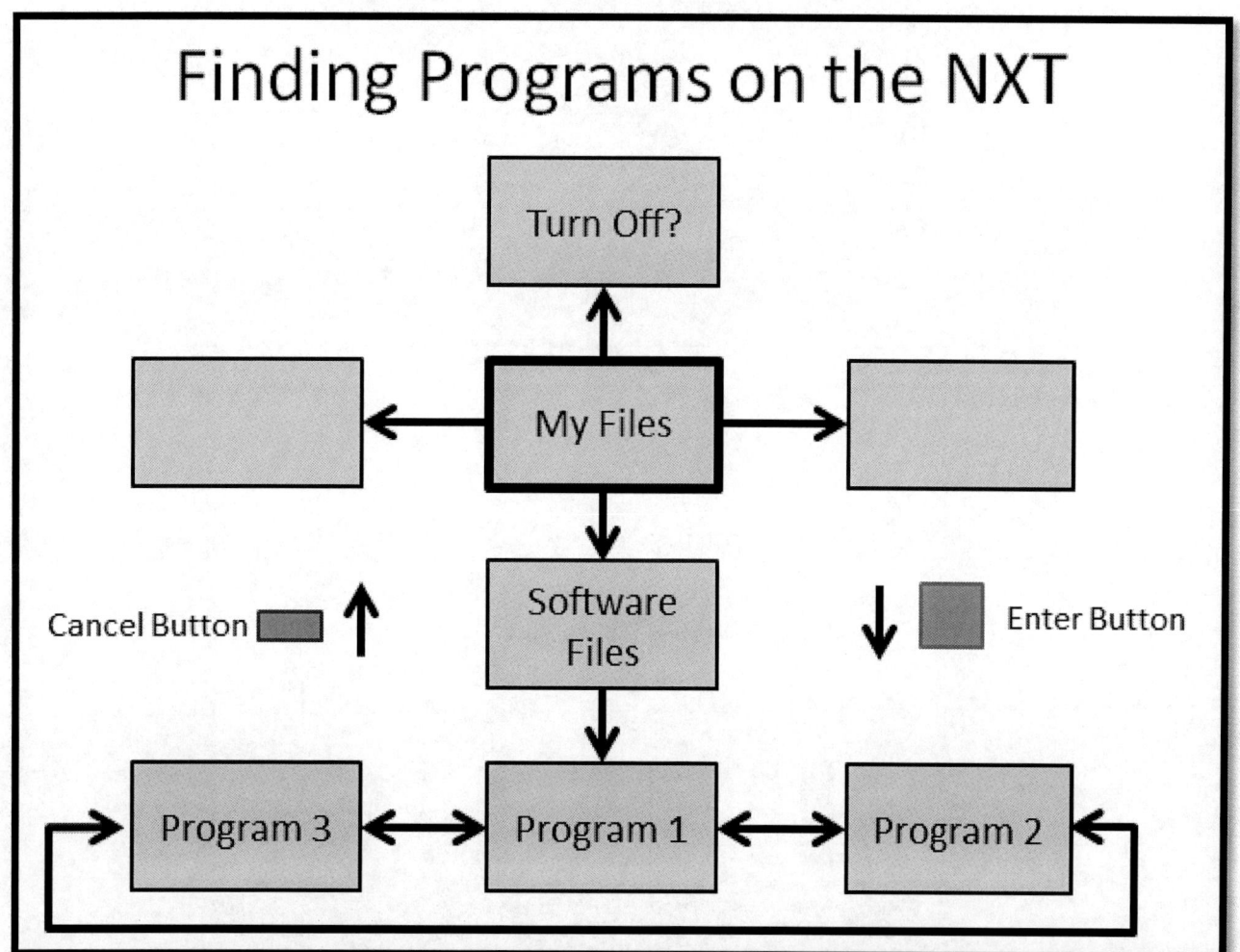

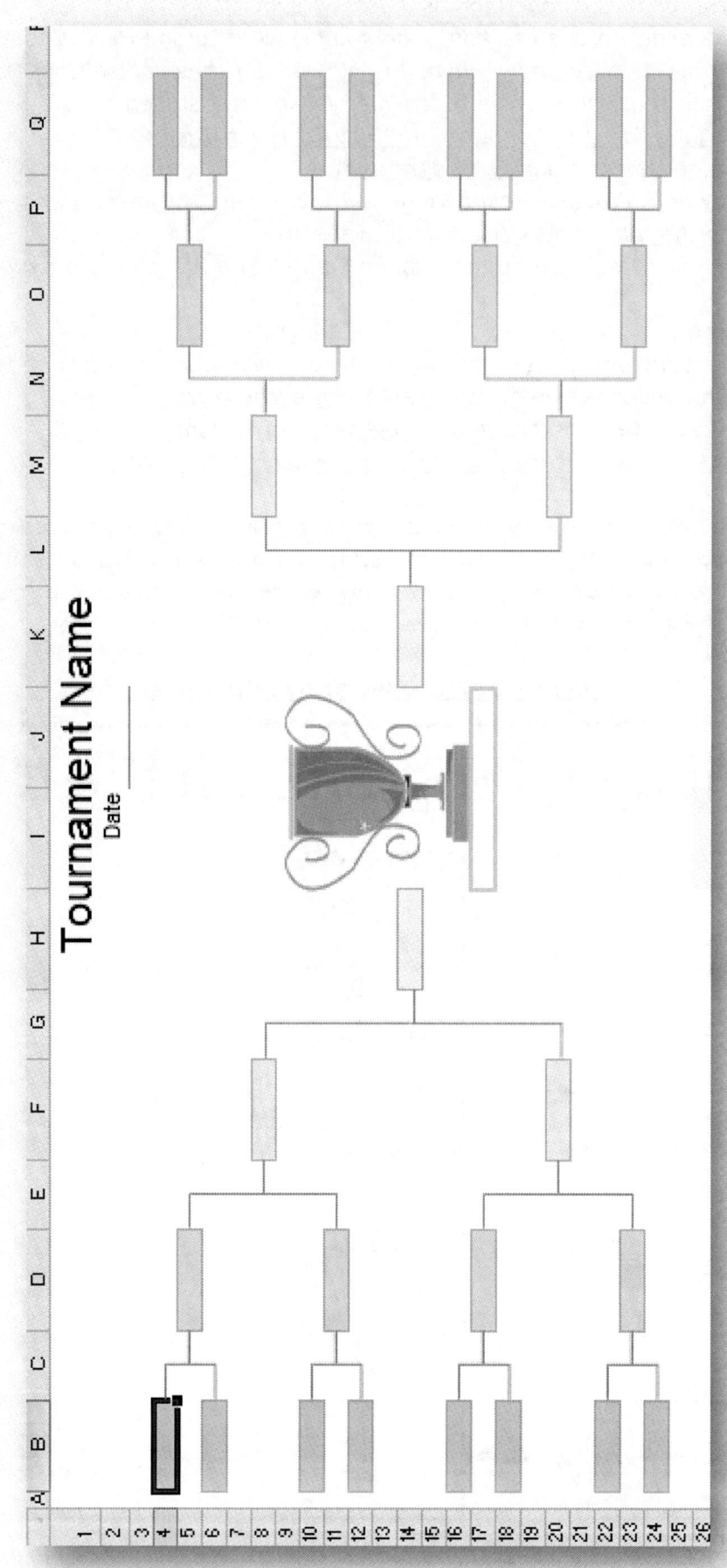

Tournament Name

Date _____

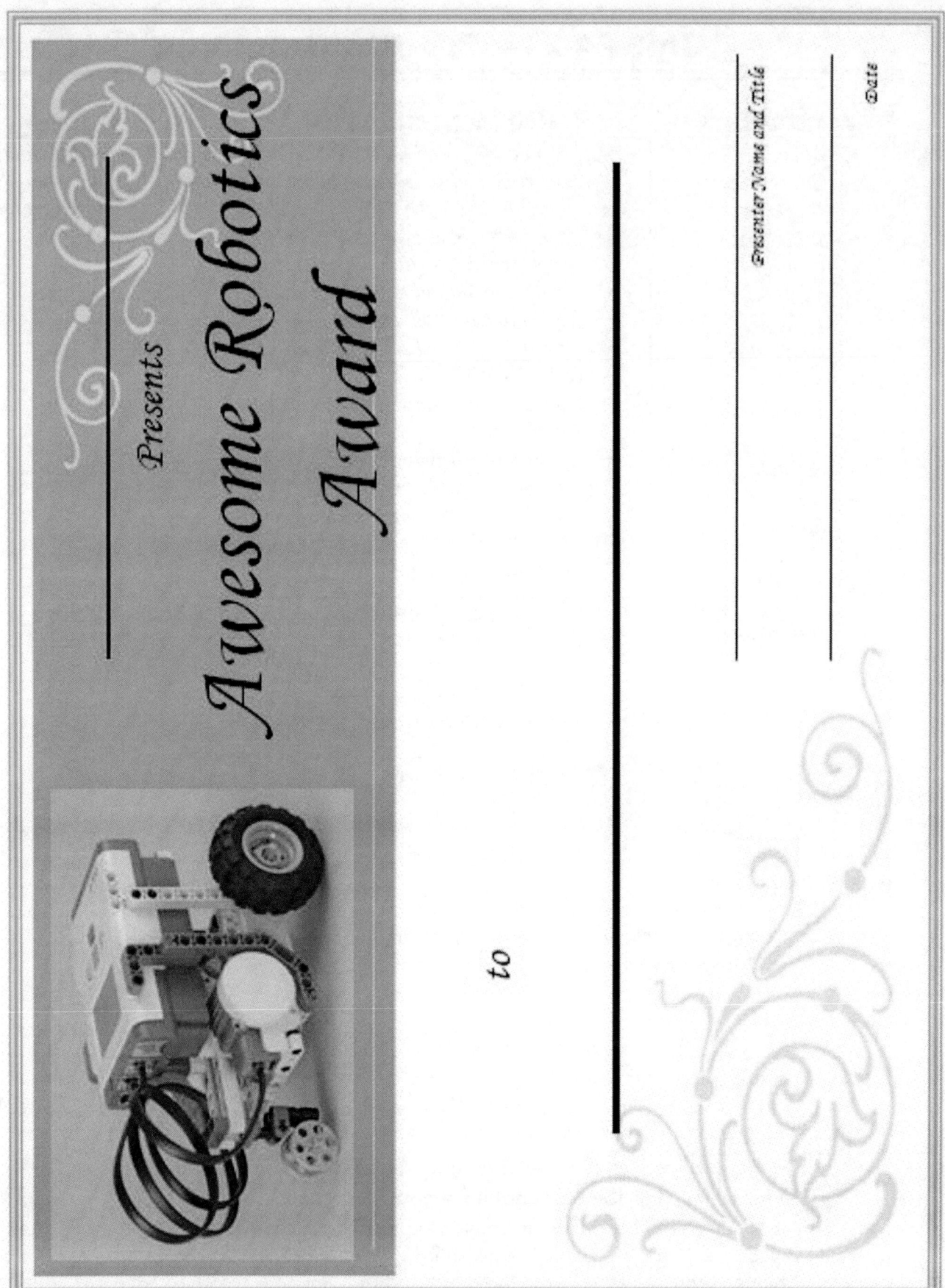

Presents

Awesome Robotics

Award

to

_____

Presenter Name and Title

_____

Date

Unit 24-27—Pre-Programming

Vocabulary	Problem solving	Big Idea
• Alice • Background • Blocks • Broadcast • Control • Costume • Debug • Green flag • Motion • Operators • Remix • Scratch • Script • Sprite • Stage • Variables	• I can't understand how to *** (Check resources, Help files, neighbors before asking teacher) • I can't remember how I *** (check scripts where you did this before) • I don't understand how to use a tool (right click and select 'help') • How do I know where scripts are (experiment) • How do I do basic skills (try Scratch Task Cards) • Is Scratch a drawing program or a presentation tool? • Can I really use someone else's script (that's 'remixing' and is encouraged in Scratch—collaborate!)	*I can learn mathematical and computational ideas while thinking creatively*
Time Required *360 minutes*	**NETS-S Standards** *3b, 4b*	**CCSS** *CCSS.Math.Practice.MP*

Essential Question
How can math be creative and collaborative?

Overview

Materials

Internet, Scratch

Teacher Preparation
- Scratch resource links on class internet start page
- Talk with subject teachers about a unit of inquiry Scratch can support
- Add Games and Education unit to class online calendar

Steps

_____Required skill level for this unit: facility with computers, an inquirer's approach to learning.

_____Circle back to whether students have used problems discussed on Problem Solving Board. Any problems they'd like to share with class?

_____Any questions from preview of programming? This can introduce the lesson.

_____'Programming' is the buzzword among middle school students. They either want to do it, or are afraid of it. What does 'programming' mean to them? Who has their own websites, YouTube channel (true—not programming, just an indicator of tech interest), blogs? Who wants to write programs and/or apps? Have they tried to? What have they used? Discuss how these exercises promote problem-solving, critical thinking, and computational thought.

_____What is <u>Scratch</u>: *A free download from MIT designed to teach pre-high school students programming basics without the techie-ness. With it, students create interactive stories, animations, games, music.*

_____Common Core alludes to programming-type skills (in <u>Standards for Mathematical Practice</u>). Tie them into Scratch:

- ***Make sense of problems and persevere in solving them***—*Scratch programs do only what they are told to do. Students must understand where they made a programming error and fix it.*
- ***Reason abstractly and quantitatively***—*Scratch programs two-dimensionally— unlike last unit's robot. To visualize process requires an abstract understanding of what is occurring.*
- ***Construct viable arguments and critique the reasoning of others***—*Scratch scripts program sprites. By downloading and remixing others' programs, students critique work of fellow students and create a better mousetrap.*
- ***Model with mathematics***—*students translate available scripts to their needs, not unlike decoding a formula in mathematics.*
- ***Use appropriate tools strategically***—*Scratch offers a plethora of scripts, blocks, tools. The trick is to adapt constructs strategically to student needs.*
- ***Attend to precision***—*To get scripts to do what students want requires patience and precision*
- ***Look for and make use of structure***—*look at available tools, scripts, blocks, options, in selecting those which facilitate student needs*
- ***Look for and express regularity in repeated reasoning***—*notice when a formula/program/script accomplishes goals.*

Best Practices

- *It is OK for students and teachers to collaborate/co-learn to achieve results*
- *Students act as co-designers of their education*
- *Students adapt a learner mentality—gain knowledge, not a grade*
- *Code is fine if project works*
- *If a student finds an elegant way to script an action, have him/her share with class*

_____Students work in groups. This is a self-paced student-directed unit. Provide a quick overview. In fact, after your screen tour, students will know 90% of what is required to complete project. As you present, encourage students to listen for the following:

- *What is background and how is it edited*
- *What is broadcasting*
- *How does one build/edit a sprite*
- *How does one add dialogue and recordings*
- *How does a sprite glide*
- *How does a sprite move forward/backward and/or flip*
- *How does one automate movement*

- *How does one wait (under control)*

_____Open Scratch on SmartScreen. Walk students around the screen, pointing out:

- *Top toolbar with tools to save/share projects*
- *Toolbar above stage where students duplicate/delete/grow/shrink their Sprite*
- *Right side of toolbar with small stage, full stage, presentation mode tools*
- *Stage*
- *Script area*
- *Sprite*
- *How to connect and activate scripts*
- *Costumes available for selected Sprite*
- *Three ways to create a Sprite*
- *Blocks—scripts that change with options*
- *Control options—great blocks there*
- *Green flag to automate scripts*
- *Programming categories (motion, looks, sound, etc.)—demonstrate each*
- *Drop-down menus available on some blocks/scripts*
- *Tabs for sprites/backgrounds that change depending upon which you're in.*

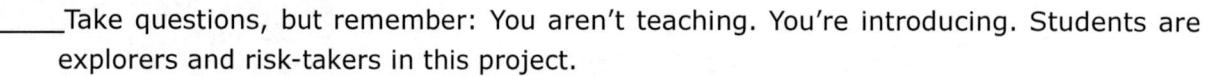

_____Take questions, but remember: You aren't teaching. You're introducing. Students are explorers and risk-takers in this project.

_____Provide a list of resources to help students find answers. Here are some I use (available with pdf. If you have print book, visit this website: http://www.protopage.com/smaatech#Untitled/Eighth_Grade):

- *Scratch main website*
- *Scratch basics*
- *Scratch lessons*
- *Intro to Scratch I*
- *Intro to Scratch II*
- *Scratch How-to Handbook*
- *Scratch video tutorials*
- *Scratch how-to cards*
- *Scratch programming tools*
- *Creating a Sprite I*

- *Create a Sprite II*
- *Import a new Sprite*
- *Moving a Sprite*
- *Animate a Sprite I*
- *Animate a Sprite II*
- *Change backgrounds*
- *Sensing and Broadcasting*
- *Broadcasting I*
- *Broadcasting II*

_____Before you help, students must try to solve their own problem. Here are strategies:

- *check resource list*
- *check Scratch website Task cards*
- *right-click on a tool and select 'help'*
- *check with a neighbor*

_____Give students time to view resource list and

Task cards, experiment with tools, explore functions before beginning project.

_____When students have practiced skills, have them create an account on Scratch website and download a Scratch project created by another 7th grader (like these—or go to http://scratch.mit.edu/latest/shared and search '7th grade'). Topic should be similar to one they will create for summative assessment. Explore how this student accomplished tasks; remix to suit project needs, then save remix to student portfolio.

_____Students will create a movie or game aligned with a class inquiry unit. For example, it could be a story that supports a history lesson or reviews a book they're reading. Give them much freedom to do in a way that works for their learning style. This is student-directed, independently-paced.

_____Have each student save completed projects to both their Scratch account and digital portfolio. Works-in-progress are saved to digital portfolios, and backed up to Google Apps account, flash drive, or emailed home via a web-based email program.

_____When project is completed, upload to Scratch, use code to embed into Blog, and write a summative post about the Scratch experience:

- *What did student like/dislike?*
- *Was it as easy/hard as student thought it would be?*
- *What problem solving skills did student use/learn?*
- *How was this alike/different from robotics?*
- *What other school projects could Scratch be used for?*

_____Visit and comment on five student blogs, following class rules for conversations:

- *Comment with relevant observations and ideas that keep discussion on topic*
- *Pose questions that elicit elaboration*
- *Respond to others' questions*
- *Acknowledge new information expressed by others and, when warranted, modify own views*

Assessment Strategies

- *Anecdotal*
- *Created Sprite*
- *Posted blog article about project (with screenshot)*
- *Completed project*
- *Tried to solve own problems*
- *Joined class discussion*

_____Remind students to transfer knowledge to classroom or home.

_____Tuck chairs under desk, headphones over tower; leave station as it was.

_____As you teach, incorporate lesson vocabulary.

Extension:

- *Discuss this quote: "What is the best method to obtain the solution to a problem? The answer is, any way that works" - Richard Feynman.*
- *Discuss this quote: "Make things as simple as possible, but not simpler." – Albert Einstein.*

- Create a Sprite from student school picture.
- Add blog progress report at the half-way point with Scratch screen shot (a formative assessment).
- Use rubric (see inset) as summative assessment. Here's link: http://scratched.media.mit.edu/resources/rubric-assessing-scratch-projects-draft-0
- Homework: Practice keyboarding with installed software, DanceMat Typing, Typing Web or Nimble Fingers (Google for website).
- Homework: Review preparatory material on 'Games and Education' for next unit.

More Information:

- Go to ScratchEd for tutorials, rubrics, assessments and more: http://scratched.media.mit.edu/
- Lesson questions? Go to http://askatechteacher.com
- Follow keyboard lessons in K-8 Keyboard Curriculum (http://structuredlearning.net/k8keyboardcurriculum.html)

If you don't get through everything, check completed items so you know what to get back to when you have time on later lessons. I find as I focus on the central idea of a lesson, clarifying questions sometimes take more time than I'd expect. I'm fine with that.

> **"Each problem that I solved became a rule which served afterwards to solve other problems."**
>
> **- Rene Descartes, "Discours de la Methode"**

Sample Scratch projects

Week 28 Gamification of Education

Vocabulary	Problem solving	Big Idea
• *Edugames* • *Flipped* • *Gaming* • *Gamification* • *Learning style* • *Reach* • *Scaffolding* • *Simulation* • *Virtual* • *Virtual world*	• *How do I undo? (Ctrl+Z)* • *My screen froze (clear a dialogue box)* • *I'm not a gamer (pick a simulation for non-gamers)* • *I'm stuck (think creatively, critically. Work as a group)* • *I don't understand (be an explorer and risk-taker)* • *Someone on my team doesn't know how to play games (help him/her)*	*Technology differentiates education in surprising ways*
Time Required *90 minutes*	**NETS-S Standards** *1b, 2a*	**CCSS** *CCSS.Math.Practice.MP*

Essential Question
How can games lead to learning?

Overview

Materials

   Internet, simulation links

Teacher Preparation
   • Talk with classroom teacher so you tie games into their conversations
   • Ensure that all required links are on lab computers
   • Add Web Communication Tools unit to class online calendar

Steps

   _____ **Required skill level for this unit: Facility with internet. Online gaming background helpful but not necessary.**

   _____ Have students had any tech problems they'd like help with?

   _____ Any questions on keyboarding?

   _____ Any questions from review of gaming and gamification of education?

   _____ What is '**Gamification' of education?** Help students come up with 'use of game design elements in educational contexts'. What are some favorites? Do they see connections between those games and education (do they learn while having fun)?

   _____ Games offer what nothing else can. Through their virtual worlds, students have the opportunity to impact events around them with no prejudice based on youth. Properly-selected games invoke problem-solving, critical thinking, logical thinking, and collaboration—all significant skills in Common Core Standards, ISTE guidelines, and 21st Century classrooms.

   _____ Common Core alludes to skills gaming (and programming like Scratch and robotics) is known for, specifically (from <u>Common Core Standards for Mathematical Practice</u>):

- **Make sense of problems and persevere in solving them**—*Students must understand the problem, understand how to solve it within the constructs of the game.*
- **Reason abstractly and quantitatively**—*students must immerse themselves in the game's environment. This requires they abstractly understand what is occurring and visualize the process.*
- **Construct viable arguments and critique the reasoning of others**—*the nature of games requires students interact with other players to succeed. They must understand the goal and discern which characters within the game can assist in its completion.*
- **Model**—*games are models of a reality students likely will never experience.*
- **Use appropriate tools strategically**—*as with real life, there are only so many tools at a player's disposal. Determine what those are and how to use them to achieve goals.*
- **Look for and make use of structure**—*a map is good. Life works better with a plan.*
- **Look for and express regularity in repeated reasoning**—*learn the rules of the community. The ones that work can be repeated.*

Best Practices--Games

- *Plan time for a learning curve*
- *Have students work in groups*
- *Be actively involved*
- *Set behavioral expectations*
- *Pick great games*
- *Align goals with learning*
- *Scaffold non-gamers*
- *Update parents consistently*
- *Demo game-ed connections*
- *If possible, invite parents in*
- *Ignore unrealistic expectations on how quickly results populate*
- *Differentiate instruction*
- *Make failure fun*
- *Fit games into class schedules*
- *Expect students to play games in many locations*
- *Include varied assessments--reflection, blogs, discussion boards*

_____Give students opportunity to 'sell' you on using their favorite game for this unit. Let them gather in small groups, themed to a game, and discuss strategies for proving the efficacy of their game for unit purposes (see above bullet list).

_____Have students present their case to class:

- *Discuss academic tie-ins—show game is more than just 'play'.*
- *Discuss student engagement, intellectual motivation, and academic reach (what does game touch; how does it appeal to different learning styles).*
- *How will control be exerted? Class must remain 'in control'.*
- *Provide citations to its effectiveness.*
- *Align selected game with standards discussed earlier in unit.*
- *Review its ease of use.*
- *Review its accessibility (do students require accounts? Are accounts free?)*

- *How much scaffolding is required for non-players?*
- *Does game encourage peer support?*

_____Students will work hard in this portion of the unit because success means they get to play their favorite game during class time (in their minds at least). This 20-30 minutes may be the most effective part of the unit.

_____When arguments are completed, 1) students vote on which games to use, 2) you assign/create groups, and then 3) students pick a game their group will play.

_____This list handles varied gaming levels of students. Include your own:

- *Bridge Builder—learn how to design and test bridges*
- *Coffee Shop—run a coffee shop business*
- *Electrocity—how does electricity contribute to the growth of communities*
- *iCivics—experience what it means to be part of a democracy*
- *Lemonade Stand—run a lemonade stand business*
- *Life (Insurance)—manage your life and see why insurance is important*
- *Making History: The Great War—WWI strategy game*
- *MidWorld Online—learn French or Spanish while completing conquests*
- *Minecraft: (links to MinecraftEdu—fee required)*
- *Mission US—students role play the American Revolution or the Civil War*
- *Past/Present—life as an American immigrant in the early 1900's*
- *Science simulations—lots of choices at 7th grade level*
- *Second Life—simulates just about anything if you can find it*
- *SimCity—learn to run a city*
- *SimTower—learn to run a skyscraper as a business*

_____Here are tasks students must accomplish, regardless of game they select:

- *Students post a start-up blog on 1) how game connects to education standards, 2) how they will be inclusive of non-gamers, 3) goals of unit.*
- *Students blog about 1) each individual's involvement, 2) connections made between game and education, 3) how education was differentiated as needed, 4) where group experienced problems and how they were solved, 5) where group experienced success and why.*
- *Students participate in Discussion Board topics you as teacher choose (based on CC Standards above).*
- *Students complete three self-assigned tasks (or a number that works for your group) that demonstrate game's educational applications. Share these in a blog post. For example, students may expect Minecraft to:*
  - *teach electricity*
  - *teach basic programming*
  - *measure gravity*
  - *create contour/topographic maps using randomly generated mountains and/or free mapping tools available*
  - *measure/evaluate area/volume by using a set number of blocks to explore how many shapes they can make with a specific area, volume, or surface area.*

A note: Some suggested games require registration, software, and/or fees. If this is not an option for your school, pick a different game or come up with a different list of game choices that satisfies your situation.

_____Suggestions for using **Bridge Builder:**

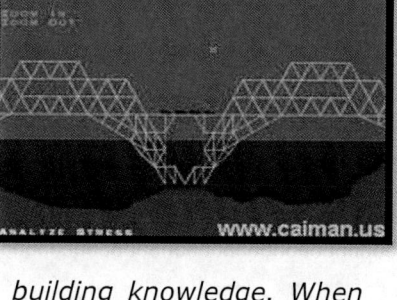

- *Students can build highly detailed bridges, landscapes and environments.*
- *There are forty levels, so students won't 'finish'. They'll blog about 'learning'.*
- *Critical thinking is required because game is as much about building as designing and testing.*
- *Uses basic physics and engineering.*
- *Have students do a pre-blog about their bridge building knowledge. When finished, blog about what they learned.*
- *Requires purchase.*

_____Suggestions for using **Coffee Shop** and **Lemonade Stand**:

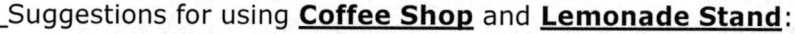

- *Preview both. Pick one.*
- *Play simulation.*
- *Track results in Excel.*
- *Evaluate data using Excel charts and graphs.*
- *Do a pre- and post-blog about student business knowledge.*
- *Optionally, create marketing materials—business cards, fliers, websites using tech skills already learned. Students can use installed programs like Word or Publisher, or online widgets like Big Huge Labs. They decide what will promote their business.*
- *Free online game, no registration required*

_____Suggestions for using **Electrocity**:

- *This game provides critical thinking and problem solving in the use/abuse of electricity, in balancing the needs of people and environment.*
- *Easy to learn, fast-moving, and keeps non-gamers' attention.*
- *Have students do a pre-blog about their knowledge on electrical use in cities. When finished, blog about what they learned.*
- *Free online game. No registration required.*

_____Suggestions for using **iCivics:**

- *Founded by Justice Sandra Day O'Connor to educate students about civics, democracy, government. For example, in We the Jury, students decide a tough case while learning what jurors discuss in deliberation room. They choose from different civil cases, analyze evidence, weigh testimony, and use appropriate arguments to reach a fair and impartial verdict.*

- *Students can play several iCivics games.*
- *Students do a pre-blog about their civics knowledge. When finished, blog about what was learned.*
- *Free online, no registration required.*

_____Suggestions for using **Life** (Insurance):

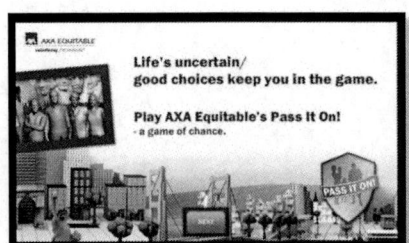

- *Life insurance isn't a topic most students are knowledgeable about so blog reflections should be especially interesting.*
- *Students do a pre-blog about their life insurance knowledge. When finished, blog about what they learned.*
- *Available in iTunes, for iPads, for free.*

_____Suggestions for using **Making History**:

- *Places student in role of national leader with power to choose their path and alter history.*
- *Students learn not just history, but international trade, religious and cultural strife, military campaigns, diplomatic negotiations.*
- *Have students do a pre-blog about their government/power knowledge. When finished, blog about what they learned.*
- *Requires purchase.*

_____Suggestions for using **MidWorld Online**:

- *Perfect for students who struggle with a foreign language.*
- *As they play, have students write their blogs in the French or Spanish they are learning.*
- *Have students do a pre-blog about their foreign language skills. When finished, blog about how it improved (or didn't).*
- *Requires purchase/registration.*

_____Suggestions for using **Minecraft**:

- *Have students establish preliminary goals of surviving, finding food, building a shelter, creating tools that allow for their survival*
- *Students can follow preset activities or create their own.*
- *Encourage collaboration among gamers to thrive in Minecraft.*

- *If your school has MinecraftEdu, expect students to participate in MinecraftEdu forums, wikis, and chats—following class's agreed-upon rules for social media interaction.*
- *Have students do a pre-blog about their knowledge of goals they established for using program. When finished, blog how that knowledge changed.*
- *Screenshot credit: Wikipedia.*
- *Requires purchase/registration for full version.*

_____Suggestions for using **Mission US**:

- *There are two games—'Crown or Colony' about American Revolution and 'Flight to Freedom' about Civil War. Both are easy.*
- *There are many reflection tools provided to encourage deeper thinking. Have students include these in their blog posts.*
- *Have students do a pre-blog about their Civil War and/or American Revolution knowledge. When finished, blog about what they learned.*
- *Requires registration; free to use.*

_____Suggestions for using **Past/Present**:

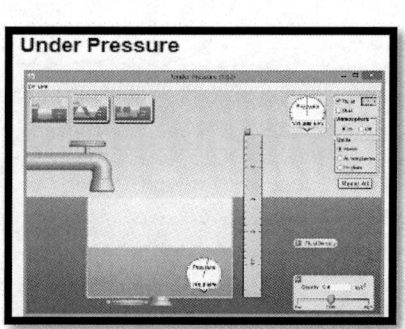

- *Designed to impart decision-making and critical thinking skills in study of American history.*
- *An interactive 3-D "virtual world" in which student "becomes" a fictional character caught up in big issues of early 1900s.*
- *Appeals to gamers as well as novices.*
- *Have students do a pre-blog about their immigrant knowledge. When finished, blog about what they learned.*
- *Requires registration; free to use; teacher accounts available.*

_____Suggestions for using **Science simulations**:

- *Lots of choices at 7th grade level. These aren't as long as other simulations, but can be tightly focused on a topic.*
- *Expect students to complete several simulations in time allotted. Have students select those that are connected thematically.*

- *Good choice for non-gamers. They will have more time to reach a comfort level with the concept of 'gamification'.*
- *Can be played online, downloaded as stand-alone, or embedded into a blog.*
- *Have students do a pre-blog about their knowledge in the area of selected simulations. When finished, blog about what they learned.*
- *Free to use online; embeddable.*

_____Suggestions for using **Second Life**:

- *Participate in a scavenger hunt that fulfills educational tasks students assign to themselves*
- *Or: Explore Greek/Roman architecture.*
- *Or: Visit five places being studied in class (i.e., art museums, Sistine Chapel, inside of a computer).*
- *Or: Use 'sandbox' to create/test/share 3D object.*
- *Or: Walk in someone else's shoes, maybe someone with a debilitating illness.*
- *Requires registration.*

_____Suggestions for using **SimTower**:

- *Find free download (this links to Abandonia).*
- *Students play this game endlessly. As they do, note what events and factors facilitate business growth/failure.*
- *Have students do a pre-blog about business of owning/operating a high-rise tower. When finished, blog about what they learned.*
- *Requires free software.*

_____Suggestions for using **SimCity:**

- *Find a free download site or buy the update—newly-aligned with ed standards. Visit SimCityEDU for information.*
- *Students can play this game endlessly. As they play, do the following:*

  - *Explore geometry concepts through building roads*
  - *Learn about energy consumption, costs and consequences. comparison of use and effects of fossil fuel, nuclear power, wind/solar energy.*
  - *Study representative government and practical, city-building issues like zoning and public works.*

- *Encourages collaboration, time management and systems thinking.*

- *Have students pre-blog about their knowledge of running a city. When finished, blog about what they learned.*
- *Requires purchase (for update).*

_____Expect gaming to be collaborative, where you as teacher learn with students. If you believe in the flipped classroom, this is a great unit.

_____Involve parents through student blogs and your open-door policy. Do not let them hear about 'games at school' through a child's casual comment. Make sure their introduction includes the game unit's structure, goals, and purpose. Invite them to play if/when possible.

_____When unit ends, reflect on it yourself: What did students accomplish? Did they experience the exhilarating sensation of learning for themselves rather than a grade?

_____Throughout class, check for understanding.

_____Remind students to transfer knowledge to classroom or home.

_____Tuck chairs under desk, headphones over tower; leave station as it was.

_____As you teach, incorporate lesson vocabulary.

Assessment Strategies

- *Anecdotal*
- *Completed project*
- *Worked well in groups*
- *Completed all blog posts*
- *Acted as teacher when necessary*
- *Developed effective arguments to support the game*

Extension:
- *Students have questions teacher can't answer? That's OK. Set up several students as 'Alpha Gamers'. Their job: to assist and answer questions.*
- *Some students don't like gaming? Like any unit of inquiry, some will like it better than others. Encourage student to get involved and give it a chance.*
- *Some students can't win at game they picked? The goal isn't winning. The goal is learning. What have they learned? Remind them that even failure has been fun. Remind them of the old adage: The only failure is when you stop trying.*
- *Tie this unit in with robotics: Have students join a virtual environment that supports concepts required for robotics, i.e., Second Life.*
- *Use Science Simulations or other science-based simulations as Minecraft resources.*
- *Extend learning by exploring how to program a simulation at Gamestart Mechanic—an online game building community for students.*
- *Have students comment on three classmate posts with suggestions/ideas.*
- *Support student gaming enthusiasm with an afterschool club. Have students complete requirements and present request to Admin (if necessary).*
- *More simulations—science oriented—at ClearLabs. They're all free.*
- *More games—Planet in Action via Google Earth.*
- *Homework: Practice keyboarding with installed software, DanceMat Typing, Typing Web or Nimble Fingers (Google name for website).*
- *Homework: Review preparatory material on 'Web Communication Tools' for next unit.*

More Information:
- *According to the Entertainment Software Association, 72 percent of American households play computer or video games. Enough said.*

- *From Engagement to Research - How Serious Can Gaming Get? PPT*
- *Best practices for using games and simulations in the classroom*
- *Minecraft resources:*

  - *http://massivelyminecraft.org/*
  - *http://minecraftedu.com/*
  - *http://youtu.be/-mTf3j2koJA*
  - *http://gamingeducators.pbworks.com/w/page/47285987/Gaming%20Educators*

- *Follow keyboard lessons in K-8 Keyboard Curriculum (http://structuredlearning.net/k8keyboardcurriculum.html)*

If you don't get through everything, check completed items so you know what to get back to when you have time on later lessons. I find as I focus on the central idea of a lesson, clarifying questions sometimes take more time than I'd expect. I'm fine with that.

> **"When you do the common things in life in an uncommon way, you will command the attention of the world."**
>
> **- George Washington Carver**

Minecraft
In school

It was lunch time on a warm spring day—the first sun of the season. Most students were outside enjoying one of the first pleasant days since the chill of winter faded. Three students came in my lab–7th graders–asking to play a program I'd never heard of called Minecraft. Their science teacher wanted them to use it as a vehicle to study minerals and geology. I knew the teacher so let them move forward and dashed off an email asking her to verify. She did.

As the students played, several 4th graders came in. "Are we allowed playing Minecraft?" Over and over. And then third graders. And fifth. To all, I said no, this was a special project for 7th grade science.

I realized I had to research this program that had so many students willing to forego the playground to sit at a computer screen with blocky retro characters who had none of the pizzazz of any other modern game. At first blush, it is about beat-em-up violence and destruction. That didn't sell me. Where was the critical thinking? The geology and minerals? I went to Common Sense Media and found it ranks Minecraft 4/5 stars with a tagline *Sandbox-style game with open online play fosters creativity.*

It goes on to say:

> *Kids can learn creative thinking, geometry, and even a little geology as they build imaginative block structures in this refreshingly open-ended mining and construction game. Given carte blanche to sculpt virtually any creation of their choice in this 3-D space, kids can try out tons of possibilities while working toward simple objectives. An option to work with others on larger building projects can help kids develop collaboration skills. Minecraft empowers players to exercise their imagination and take pride in their digital creations as they learn basic building concepts.*

Subjects covered include:
- Math: estimation, geometry, shapes
- Science: geology, rocks and minerals
- Hobbies: building

…and skills taught:
- *Thinking & Reasoning: defining problems, hypothesis-testing, problem solving*

- *Creativity: imagination, making new creations, producing new content*
- *Collaboration: cooperation, group projects, teamwork*

I'd read enough. I decided to declare Monday and Friday lunches 'Minecraft Mania'. I would watch, observe, make sense of all the excitement.

Word got out and my lab was packed those two lunch hours—all year. As I watched my students play, I saw lots of the thinking and risk-taking we encourage in traditional educational venues. Students rattled off fifteen-digit IP addresses that allowed others to join their game, created servers to compete against each other, strategized how to reach their goals, formed alliances with other players, researched solutions on the internet, shared with each other so everyone could participate (the program requires a fee, but that didn't stop any one).

Is there something to this?

I polled my PLN and got no supporters. I might have given up, but ran across this article, _Learn to Play: Minecraft in the classroom._ And then these teaching wikis about educational uses of Minecraft, _Welcome to the Minecraft in School Wiki!_ and _Gaming Educators._ There's also an edition of Minecraft specifically for schools called MinecraftEdu.

As I was putting this review to bed, I came across ECOO 2012 who had a packed seminar on Minecraft in education. Among the benefits of playing this game:

- *peer learning*
- *sharing computers*
- *co-operative play*
- *parallel play*
- *exploring*
- *testing theories*
- *developing hypotheses*
- *negotiating social agreements*

I can't think of another educational program that does so much in so little space with so many avid followers. Can you?

Week 29-32 Web Communication Tools

Vocabulary	Problem solving	Big Idea
• *Animoto* • *Blog* • *Brainstorm* • *Embed* • *GIF* • *Jing* • *MindMap* • *Prezi* • *Publish* • *QR code* • *Screencast* • *Screenshot* • *Scribd* • *Share* • *Shelfari* • *Voice Thread* • *Voki* • *Web 2.0* • *Widget*	• *I don't know how to embed a tool* • *Where's embed code? (search screen)* • *I see 'share' (click that)* • *I like the tool, but it charges a fee (look around for free version)* • *My typing disappeared (Ctrl+Z)* • *How do I undo? (Ctrl+Z)* • *What's the difference between 'save' and 'save-as'?* • *My screen froze (clear dialogue box)* • *Log-in doesn't work (did you type it correctly?)* • *How do I save when there's no 'save' button? (try a screen shot)* • *I don't like the tool we're looking at (try a different one)* • *Which tool should I use? (which works best for your goals?)* • *I don't understand tool (ask teammates for help)*	*Use technology to diversify and differentiate communication so all listeners understand*
Time Required 360 minutes	**NETS-S Standards** 1b, 2a	**CCSS** *CCSS.ELA-Literacy.SL.7.5*

Essential Question
How do I use technology to differentiate communicate?

Overview

Materials

Internet, links to Web communication tools

Teacher Preparation
- Talk with classroom teacher so Web communication tools list includes those teacher considers important to inquiry
- Ensure required links are on lab computers
- Review what worked best last year and what new tools are available this year
- Test all tools so you know which require log-ins, emails, and which students can use as a 'guest' or with a throw-away email address

Steps

_____**Required skill level for this unit: Internet basics, inquiring mind, experience presenting to a group.**

_____Circle back on Problem Solving Board. Any tech problems students need help with?

_____Any questions on keyboarding?

_____Discuss 'online communication'. It:

- *Is a way to collaborate and publish employing digital environments and media (think: Google Apps)*
- *Is a way to communicate information and ideas to multiple audiences (think: widgets, embeds, websites)*
- *Develops cultural understanding and global awareness (think: blogs, forums)*
- *Enables students to contribute as a team (think: Google Apps, wikis)*
- *Includes email, forums, blogs, social media, ????*
- *Integrates information from different media to develop a comprehensive understanding of an issue (think: blogs, websites, Animoto)*
- *Is a way to consult research materials*
- *Is a way to pose questions, elaborate on discussions, and respond to others' comments with relevant ideas*
- *Is a way for students to integrate new information into their views*

_____The goal of this lesson is to broaden student understanding of available communication tools. What they have used (MS Word, Excel, PowerPoint) is but a fraction of what can be used to communicate ideas. The good news is—many tools are intuitive to learn, free, and require nominal log-in information (suitable for pre-teen and teen users).

_____The list you develop for this unit should represent a variety of learning styles (art, music, color, words). This is a great opportunity to differentiate instruction.

_____This Unit works best if students are working toward a final project that requires them to collaboratively investigate, draw conclusions, share, and publish. Talk with class teachers to identify such a topic. Some tools that have worked for my classes are:

- o *Alice (free download at http://www.alice.org/)—program a game/video in a 3D environment and embed into digital portfolio. This is a preview for 8th grade—anyone want to take it on?*
- o *Animoto (free online use; fee for premier account)—use photos and videos, mix with music and words, to create an amazing video on any topic.*
- o *Big Huge Labs (free online use)—do cool stuff with digital photos like magazine covers, pop art poster, map maker, movie poster, a badge, a calendar, a picture cube, wallpaper, trading cards, comicizer, a billboard, a blog header, and more. Can be used in conjunction with another tool.*
- o *Bubbl.us (free online use)—brainstorm with classmates to create a project. There are a lot of mind map options (try SpicyNodes). Can be used in conjunction with another tool.*
- o *Class Tools (free online)—includes many options to share knowledge like Venn Diagrams, animated books, a fake Facebook/Twitter, Learning Cycle.*
- o *Comic Creators (most free; some require registration)—communicate with comics. Links go to my favorites:*

  - *Arthur Comic Creator—PBS's version of this writing genre*
  - *Comics (Newspapers and Posters, too)—easy to use, but limited*
  - *Lego Comic Builder—uses Legos*
  - *Zimmer Twins—my favorite*

- *Comic Creator—Disney*
- *Comic creator—Bubblr*

- *Crossword Puzzles (free online)—test knowledge with a popular quiz format. Can be used in conjunction with another tool.*
- *Diagrams Online (free online; fee for more than five)—create popular diagrams: flowcharts, floor plans, technical drawings and more.*
- *Equiz (free online)—create, take and grade custom quizzes online.*
- *GIF Creator (free online)—create GIF-length movie. Be creative!*
- *Glogster (free online)—create a poster and embed it into a digital portfolio.*
- *Go Animate! (free online)—create an animated lesson to teach classmates whatever you want—like how to use this tool.*
- *Google Map Maker (free online)—create personalized maps.*
- *Jing (free online)—make screenshots and screencasts.*
- *Museum Box (free online)—collect evidence (pictures, videos, music, more) in 'boxes' that students can pick based on their interest level.*
- *Poll Daddy (free online)—Surveys—use same online tool used for class poll of classmate interests. What do you want to know?*
- *Prezi (free online)—organize and share ideas with this visual presentation tool.*
- *Publish Magazines online (free online; fee for premier)*
- *QR Codes (free online)—most only options are free. Pick one that allows students to code URLs and text—and embed in blogs.*
- *Shelfari (free online)—so many opportunities to use Shelfari. Make a class library, add book reviews for next year's class, even add QR codes with book information.*

50 Ways to Tell a Story	Comic Creators	Google Map Maker	Puzzle Maker	Slideshows online
		MindMaps		
Animoto	Crossword Puzzle Creator	Museum Box	QR Codes	Timelines
Big Huge Labs	GIF Creator	**Photostory** / Poll Daddy	Screen Cast	Vokis
Class Tools	Glogster	Prezi	Shelfari	Widget Creator
	Go Animate!			

- *Slideshows Online (free online; fee for premier)—Slideshare, Slideboom. Kizoa is only option that lets you create and share online—the rest need a slideshow you upload.*
- *Tagxedo (free online)—evaluate words. Students enter book report, thoughts on a topic, whatever they choose, then select colors and shape to enhance message.*
- *Timelines (free online)—pick from five options to create timelines online. Most require accounts, some require email validation.*
- *Voice Thread—communicate by recording. This is a collaborative, interactive, multimedia slide show that holds images, documents, and videos.*
- *Vokis (free online)—create speaking avatars that communicate ideas.*
- *Wolfram Alpha widgets (http://www.wolframalpha.com/widgets/) (free online)—create/share widgets and embed into digital portfolio.*
- *?????—what new Web tool do your students like?*

_____A table (see below) is helpful. Embed it into class wiki or blog. Each topic can be linked to a separate page with instructions and training videos. Click inset above for example of my Web Communication Tool wiki page. I find it easier to create it in advance and let students click through choices and how-tos to make their selection. You may do it differently. The goal: student directed, multi-media communication.

Alice	Crossword Puzzles	MindMaps	Puzzle Maker	Timelines
Animoto	Diagrams Online	Google MapMaker	QR Codes	Voice Thread
Big Huge Labs	Equizzer	Museum Box	Screen Cast/Jing	Vokis
Bubbl.us	GIF Creator	Poll Daddy Surveys	Shelfari	Widget Creator
ClassTools	Glogster	Prezi	Slideshows Online	?????
Comic Creator	Go Animate	Publish Magazine	Tagxedo	

_____A few notes:

- *Some options link to a brief, explanatory video so students can get a sense of the difficulty of the tool (but not all).*
- *Some link to multiple programs that accomplish same goal (i.e., Timelines). Students can pick whichever suits them.*

_____Students work in groups of three. Sign up for presentation week and tool. This can be done using wall signs (see end of Unit) or an online program like Sign Up Genius (Google for address). Have each student take a reminder stub (see end of Unit) with group member names, group lead, date of presentation, and Web 2.0 tool they will present.

_____Review each tool for about 1 minute, then give students time to make a decision and sign up.

_____Remind students of the online widget they used at beginning of course—PollDaddy.

_____Review project grading rubric on SmartScreen. Explain what each factor means and take student questions.

_____Give students one class to research, organize team, before presentations begin.

_____During presentation, one student will teach while others walk around and help classmates. Teacher will observe. Students must be critical thinkers and problem solvers.

_____During presentation, students cover:

- *how to use tool*
- *how tool communicates ideas*
- *how to create a project*

Best Practices

- *It is OK for students and teachers to collaborate, both co-learners with the same goal*
- *Avoid web tools with too much advertising*
- *Resist urge to 'teach'. Expect students to self-teach, using critical thinking skills and problem solving tools honed throughout year*

- *how to troubleshoot*
- *how to embed project into blogs*
- *what students learned from tool*

_____Each presentation will take about thirty minutes. When students are done, group posts an example (embed or screenshot), directions, and a reflection to their blog.

_____Done? Retake poll from beginning of class. Review each unit briefly. Which was their favorite? Discuss results. Did anything change? Any surprises (i.e., pre-programming was easier than expected).

_____Throughout class, expect students to solve problems and make decisions.

_____Remind students to transfer knowledge to classroom or home.

_____Tuck chairs under desk, headphones over tower; leave station as it was.

_____As you teach, incorporate lesson vocabulary.

Assessment Strategies

- *Anecdotal*
- *Worked well in group*
- *Completed project; graded*
- *Voted on coursework poll*

Extension:
- *Post 'Am I ready?' sheets online as a reminder a week before presentation begin.*
- *Have students add their presentation date to class calendar (embedded into class blog or website).*
- *Those who finish each week can vote in PollDaddy poll.*
- *Those who finish each week can upload projects to blog posts.*

More Information:
- *For summer ideas, read article at end of unit, "7 Digital Ways to End the School Year"*
- *Lesson questions? Go to http://askatechteacher.com*

WEB TOOL SIGN-UP

I am the GROUP Contact:_____

My GROUP is:_____

Our Web 2.0 Tool is:_____

Our presentation date is:_____

Sign-up Sheet
Web Tool You-Teach Presentations

	Class #1	Class #2	Class #3
Week of _____	#1	#1	#1
	#2	#2	#2
	#3	#3	#3
Week of _____	#1	#1	#1
	#2	#2	#2
	#3	#3	#3
Week of _____	#1	#1	#1
	#2	#2	#2
	#3	#3	#3
Week of _____	#1	#1	#1
	#2	#2	#2
	#3	#3	#3
Week of _____	#1	#1	#1
	#2	#2	#2
	#3	#3	#3
Week of _____	#1	#1	#1
	#2	#2	#2
	#3	#3	#3
Week of _____	#1	#1	#1
	#2	#2	#2
	#3	#3	#3
Week of _____	#1	#1	#1
	#2	#2	#2
	#3	#3	#3

	Class #1	Class #2	Class#3
Animoto—turn pic into movies	#1	#1	#1
	#2	#2	#2
	#3	#3	#3
Big Huge Labs—present info	#1	#1	#1
	#2	#2	#2
	#3	#3	#3
Bubbl.us—mind map	#1	#1	#1
	#2	#2	#2
	#3	#3	#3
ClassTools—many options	#1	#1	#1
	#2	#2	#2
	#3	#3	#3
Crossword Puzzle Creator	#1	#1	#1
	#2	#2	#2
	#3	#3	#3
Electrocity—edutainment game	#1	#1	#1
	#2	#2	#2
	#3	#3	#3
Glogster—online poster	#1	#1	#1
	#2	#2	#2
	#3	#3	#3
Poll Daddy—polls on topics	#1	#1	#1
	#2	#2	#2
	#3	#3	#3
Puzzle Maker—test yourself	#1	#1	#1
	#2	#2	#2
	#3	#3	#3
QR Codes—hide info	#1	#1	#1
	#2	#2	#2
	#3	#3	#3
Shelfari—book collection	#1	#1	#1
	#2	#2	#2
	#3	#3	#3
Timelines—with pics, vids.	#1	#1	#1
	#2	#2	#2
	#3	#3	#3
Vokis—talking avatars	#1	#1	#1
	#2	#2	#2
	#3	#3	#3
Wolfram Alpha widgets	#1	#1	#1
	#2	#2	#2
	#3	#3	#3
Zimmer Twins—comic creator	#1	#1	#1
	#2	#2	#2
	#3	#3	#3

Web-based Communication Tools Assessment

*Student name*_____

*Teacher name*_____

*Points (see reverse side for comments*_____

CATEGORY	Exemplary—4 points	Developing—2 points	Unsatisfactory—0 points	RATING
Knowledge of selected tool **8 points**	Demonstrates clear understanding of how to use tool including terminology and tool website. Shows evidence of preparation for both group teaching and classmate problem-solving. Understanding is student-initiated with minimal assistance from teacher. Displays enthusiasm for tool and appreciation for its part in the learning experience. *When applicable, can show class how to embed completed tool into class blog. Knows which 'widget' to use and is able to help when classmates have difficulties.*	Demonstrates mixed understanding of tool. Shows some evidence of preparation for both teaching and problem-solving. Requires teacher assistance more than once. Displays some confidence in knowledge, enthusiasm for tool, and appreciation for its part in the learning experience. *Has some difficulty showing class how to embed completed tool into class blog or wiki page. Hasn't sufficiently prepared prior to teaching.*	Demonstrates a murky understanding of selected tool with little evidence of preparation for teaching or problem-solving. Requires substantial assistance from others to complete presentation. Displays lack of confidence in ability to make tool part in learning experience. *Unable to show class how to embed tool into class blog and/or wiki page.*	/8
Ability to teach students **4 points**	Demonstrates how to use tool in an authentic, personal, and enthusiastic manner. Uses terms class understands. Speaks slowly and clearly so class can complete steps. Provides trouble shooting and problem-solving tips (discovered as student learned to use tool).	Has some difficulty teaching students to use tool. Teaching lacks confidence and doesn't always engage students. Sometimes speaks too quickly for class to follow and some students are unable to complete project. Occasionally unable to trouble-shoot or problem-solve.	Has considerable difficulty teaching students. Teaching lacks confidence and doesn't engage students. Unable to trouble-shoot and problem-solve when asked. Students are unable to complete project.	/4
Reflection on tool's usefulness **4 points**	Reminds students how tool can be used to communicate the theme with examples. Fully addresses student questions about how to accomplish this. Reflection on blog is authentic and original, displays thoughtful analysis, and includes goals for continued learning.	Doesn't remind students of tool's usefulness, but provides examples. Is able to address some questions. Blog reflection shows insufficient original thought and incomplete itemization of goals for continued learning.	Reflection doesn't describe tool's use for class theme, shows little original thought, and does not include goals for continued learning.	/4
Group Work **4 points**	Consistently works toward group goals. Display sensitivity to feelings of others and values all members.	Sometimes works toward group goals. Is at times insensitive to the feelings of others.	Never works toward group goals or contributes. Is not sensitive to the feelings and needs of others in the group.	/4

Am I Ready

For Web Communications Tool Presentation

Do I know how the tool works	
Do I know the problems/trouble-shooting	
Can I embed it into wiki page	
Can I reflect on this tool	
Can I tie it into class theme	
Am I participating fully in my group	

Notes:

_____

_____

_____

Am I Ready

For Web Communications Tool Presentation

Do I know how the tool works	
Do I know the problems/trouble-shooting	
Can I embed it into wiki page	
Can I reflect on this tool	
Can I tie it into class theme	
Am I participating fully in my group	

Notes:

_____

_____

_____

PS

If you teach technology, it's likely you're a geek. Even if you didn't start out that way–say, you used to be a first grade teacher and suddenly your Admin in their infinite wisdom, moved you to the tech lab—you became a geek. You morphed into the go-to person for tech problems, computer quirks, crashes and freezes.

Overnight, your colleagues assumed you received an upload of data that allowed you to Know the answers to   their every techie question. It didn't matter that yesterday, you were one of them. Now, you are on a pedestal, their necks craned upward as they ask you, *How do I get the SmartScreen to work?* or *We need the microphones working for a lesson I'm starting in three minutes. Can you please-please-please fix them?*

Celebrate your cheeky geekiness. Flaunt it for students and colleagues. Play Minecraft. That's you now–you are sharp, quick-thinking. You tingle when you see an iPad. You wear a flash drive like jewelry. The first thing you do when you get to school is check your email

It's OK. Here at Structured Learning and Ask a Tech Teacher, we understand. The readers understand. You're at home. To honor you, we've created these two posters (see next pages). They provide more ways to get your geek fully on as you go through your day.

7 Digital Ways to End the School Year

If you've been swearing all year to get students online using some of those amazing digital tools. I have some ideas for you. These seven projects will be so much fun, they will eagerly welcome the new school year, hoping you have more toys for them to learn.

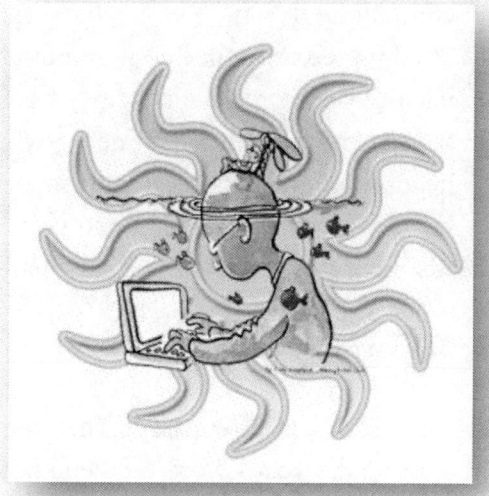

The trick with so many of these online sites is: Let students explore. Don't rush them. Don't teach them every twist and turn. Don't expect perfection. Expect inquiry and enthusiasm and self-paced discovery. Let them solve problems as they create.

Here are seven ideas for amazing end-of-year projects that leave students thinking the school year is ending too soon:

End-of-year Multimedia Summative

Students take pictures of each other holding up favorite projects or working on tech skills—humorously, of course. Use these pictures in an <u>Animoto</u> movie to share light-hearted details of their Year in Tech. Open it with a magazine cover of student (created in <u>Big Huge Labs</u>). Accessorize with music, transitions, and text bubbles. Save to class network and load onto the school set of iPads. Students can play these movies on the last day of class as they celebrate the end of school. If you don't have iPads, gather students in comfortable seating, play a student video as they reflect on another successful year of Tech.

Tips and Tricks Trading Cards

Create **trading cards** (in <u>Big Huge Labs</u>) for next year's students that share grade-level hints and tips about thriving in tech class

Voki Cheerleader

Create a **<u>Voki</u>** that will greet next year's students with attaboys when they most need it—*you can do it—just two more minutes of typing! You are blazing! And you almost never look at your fingers—woah!*

Introductory Movie

Create a movie of the school for prospective students. Walk around the campus sharing what goes on in the gym, the science lab, lockers. It should be upbeat and positive, underscoring activities that make the school a uniquely great learning environment

Digital Welcome Book

Create a digital 'Welcome' book, telling next year's new students how to keep track of log-ins, what the computer UN and PW is, the best approach to keyboarding, when Minecraft Mania time is, and anything else you decide is important for new students. Maybe do the Classroom tour that the teacher usually does on the first day of school. Walk around the classroom pointing out where the bulletin boards are with important news, what the 'Evidence Board' is, how to use the printer, where to get new headphones/pencils if yours disappear—which are the best headphones. Tape this as a movie that can be played on an iPad. Next year students will each receive an iPad at the classroom door with instructions on how to activate their student-guided tour.

Jeopardy Summative

Play Tech Class Jeopardy! There are a lot of online templates for Jeopardy. Simply use questions that sum up the year's worth of tech knowledge or take the questions from the students. What do they think was most important? Divide the class into teams, give them study guides to prepare. While they study, you create the game slides, and then play on the last day. An alternative to this is to have each team create their own Jeopardy game, with questions of their choice, and spend 15 minutes on each game—see who wins.

Summer Padlet

Put up a Padlet (the new name for Wallwisher) on the class website, blog or wiki (in my case, the class internet start page) inviting all students to add notes about what they're doing this summer. Keep these up all summer, until the new school year. Students can check in while on vacation and add notes for classmates about what they ended up doing even though they planned something else.

10 To become A BETTER

steps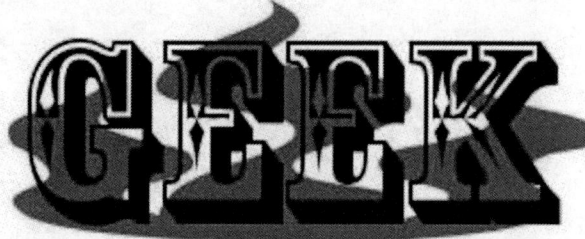

1. Use **Tech**
2. Use **it** every day--save some trees
3. Use **it** when it seems difficult
4. Use **it** in class--and at home
5. Use **Tech** now--right now
6. Use **it** instead of something else
7. Teach a friend to use **it**
8. Teach a lot of friends to use **it**
9. Make **it** your first choice
10. Keep using **it**

15 ways To GET YOUR GEEK ON

1.   Be smart. Yeah, it feels good
2.   That's my inner Geek speaking
3.   Think. Exercise your brain.
4.   Waves. Sigh.
5.   Keep repeating, *People are my friends.* Like Siri.
6.   Move away from the keyboard--Not.
7.   Some people watch TV. I play with a Rubik's Cube
8.   Be patient. I'm buffering.
9.   There must be a shortkey for that
10. Life needs an Undo key
11. Leave me alone for 2 minutes and I'll go to sleep
12. Yes, I can fix your computer
13. Like a computer, I do what you tell me to
14. My RAM is full. Come back later.
15. Slow down. My processor isn't that fast

Index

SL Technology Books for your Classroom

Which book?	Price (print/digital/Combo)	How Many?
Kindergarten-5th Tech Textbook (each)	$29.99/23.99/48.58 + p&h	
6th Grade Tech Textbook	$31.99/23.99/50.38 + p&h	
K-6 Combo (all 7 textbooks)	$190.74/151.14/341.87 + p&h	
35 More Projects for K-6 (aligned w cur)	$31.99/25.99/52.18 + p&h	
55 Tech Projects—Volume I or Volume II	$36.99/$24.99/$55.99 + p&h	
Volume I/II Combo	$66.99/$44.99/$111.97 + p&h	
K-8 Keyboard Curriculum	$29.95/23.99/48.55 + p&h	
K-8 Digital Citizenship Curriculum	$29.95/23.99/48.55 + p&h	
K-5 Common Core Lesson	$29.95/23.99/48.58 + p&h	
38 Web 2.0 Articles	$6.99 (digital only)	
16 Holiday Projects	$14.99 (digital only) + p&h	
19 Posters for the Tech Lab	$6.99 (digital only)	
18 More Posters for the Tech Lab	$12.99 (digital only)	
98 Tech Tips From Classroom	$9.99 (digital only)	
760+ Websites to Kick start Tech Ed	$14.99 (digital only)	
K-5 Tech Scope and Sequences	$14.99 (digital only)	
New Teacher Survival Kit (K-5)	$338.21/284.28/563.51+ p&h	
New Teacher Survival Kit (K-6)	$370.20/308.27/613.90 + p&h	
New Teacher Survival Kit (6-8)	$282.83/252.87/408.78 + p&h	
Bundles of lesson plans	$7.99 and up	
Mentoring (1 hr. at a time)	$50/hr.	
Year-long tech curriculum help (via wiki)	$100	
Consulting/seminars/webinars	Call or email for prices	
	Total	

Fill out this form (prices subject to change).
Email Zeke.rowe@structuredlearning.net.
Pay via PayPal, Amazon, TPT, pre-approved school
    district PO.
Questions? Contact Zeke Rowe

Structured Learning
Premiere Provider of Technology Teaching Books to the Education Community